ONE DAY.....

I'M GOING TO BE

AWESOME

THE PROCRASTINATOR'S GUIDE TO OVERCOMING PERFECTIONISM

ALEXANDER WELLINGTON

ONE DAY...
I'M GOING TO BE
AWE SOME

THE PROCRASTINATOR'S GUIDE TO OVERCOMING PERFECTIONISM

ALEXANDER WELLINGTON

TABLE OF CONTENTS

CHAPTER ONE
INTRODUCTION TO PROCRASTINATION
Focus: Causes and Consequences

Procrastination. The word alone carries a weight, a sense of guilt, and sometimes even shame. But what exactly is procrastination? Is it simply laziness, a lack of motivation, or something more complex?

At its core, procrastination is the act of delaying or postponing tasks, often until the last possible moment. It's the art of putting off today what could be done tomorrow, and tomorrow becomes the next day, and so on, until deadlines loom large and stress levels skyrocket. But for many, procrastination goes deeper than simply avoiding work; it's intertwined with perfectionism, fear of failure, and a desire for control.

Picture this: you have an important project due in a week. You know you should start working on it, but instead, you find yourself scrolling mindlessly through social media, cleaning your apartment for the fifth time this week, or binge-watching your favorite TV show. Sound familiar? Welcome to the world of procrastination.

But why do we procrastinate? The reasons are as varied as the individuals who engage in this behavior. For some, it's a coping mechanism, a way to avoid the anxiety and pressure that come with tackling a daunting task. For others, it's a way to maintain a sense of control; if we wait until the last minute, we can blame our lack of time rather than our abilities if things don't turn out perfectly.

Procrastination is not a new phenomenon. In fact, it's been documented throughout history, with famous figures like Leonardo da Vinci and Mark Twain known for their procrastination tendencies. Even the ancient Greeks recognized the allure of procrastination, with the word "akrasia" used to describe the state of acting against one's better judgment.

In today's fast-paced world, where distractions are constant and expectations are high, procrastination has become more prevalent than ever. With the rise of technology, we have access to endless sources of entertainment and information, making it all too easy to procrastinate with just a few clicks or taps.

But procrastination is not just a harmless habit; it can have serious consequences. From missed deadlines and poor performance to strained relationships and increased stress, the effects of procrastination can permeate every aspect of our lives. And yet, despite knowing the potential repercussions, many of us continue to procrastinate, trapped in a cycle of avoidance and regret.

One of the biggest challenges of overcoming procrastination is understanding the mindset behind it. For many procrastinators, perfectionism plays a significant role. We hold ourselves to impossibly high standards, fearing that anything less than perfection is failure. As a result, we put off starting a task until we feel confident that we can do it flawlessly, which, of course, rarely happens.

But perfectionism isn't the only driving force behind procrastination. Fear of failure also plays a significant role. We worry that if we try our best and still fall short, it will confirm our worst fears about our abilities. So instead of facing the possibility of failure head-on, we delay taking action, convincing ourselves that we'll do better tomorrow, next week, or next month.

The irony of procrastination is that while we may think we're avoiding failure, we're actually setting ourselves up for it. By putting off important tasks, we deprive ourselves of the time and resources needed to do our best work, increasing the likelihood of subpar results.

But procrastination isn't just about avoiding failure; it's also about seeking control. By delaying tasks until the last minute, we maintain a sense of power over our lives, even if it's just an illusion. We tell ourselves that we work best under pressure, that we thrive on the adrenaline rush of a looming deadline. And while it's true that some people do perform well under pressure, for many procrastinators, this mindset only serves to perpetuate the cycle of procrastination.

So how do we break free from the grip of procrastination? How do we overcome the fear of failure, the allure of perfectionism, and the need for control? The journey to becoming less of a procrastinator and more of a proactive, productive individual begins with understanding the underlying causes of our procrastination and learning effective strategies for managing it.

In the chapters that follow, we'll explore the psychology of procrastination, examine its consequences, and delve into practical techniques for overcoming it. We'll uncover the root causes of procrastination, identify common patterns and triggers, and learn how to cultivate habits that promote productivity and success.

But most importantly, we'll discover that procrastination doesn't have to define us. We have the power to change our habits, reframe our mindset, and reclaim control over our lives. So let's embark on this journey together, knowing that with dedication, perseverance, and a healthy dose of self-compassion, we can overcome procrastination and unleash our full potential.

CHAPTER TWO
THE PSYCHOLOGY OF PROCRASTINATION
Focus: Roots and Types

In the previous chapter, we explored the concept of procrastination and its various manifestations in our lives. Now, let's delve deeper into the psychology behind procrastination. Why do we procrastinate, and what factors contribute to this seemingly irrational behavior?

At its core, procrastination is a complex interplay of psychological, emotional, and situational factors. Understanding these factors is crucial to unraveling the mystery of procrastination and developing effective strategies for overcoming it.

The Roots of Procrastination

Procrastination often stems from a combination of intrinsic and extrinsic factors. Intrinsic factors refer to internal beliefs, attitudes, and personality traits that influence our behavior, while extrinsic factors are external circumstances and environmental influences.

Intrinsic Factors:

1. **Fear of Failure:** One of the most common reasons for procrastination is the fear of failure. When we doubt our abilities or worry about not meeting expectations, we may

avoid starting a task altogether to protect ourselves from the possibility of failure.

2. **Perfectionism:** Perfectionists are particularly prone to procrastination. They set impossibly high standards for themselves and fear that anything less than perfect will be deemed a failure. As a result, they may delay starting a task until they feel confident they can achieve perfection.

3. **Low Self-Efficacy:** Individuals with low self-efficacy, or a lack of confidence in their abilities, may procrastinate because they doubt their capacity to succeed. They may feel overwhelmed by the task at hand and believe they lack the skills or resources to complete it successfully.

4. **Impulsivity:** Some people procrastinate due to impulsivity, a tendency to act without thinking through the consequences. They may prioritize immediate gratification over long-term goals, succumbing to distractions and procrastinating on important tasks.

5. **Lack of Motivation:** A lack of motivation can also lead to procrastination. When we don't feel inspired or passionate about a task, we may struggle to muster the energy and enthusiasm needed to get started.

Extrinsic Factors:

1. **Task Aversion:** Procrastination can also be driven by aversion to the task itself. If a task is perceived as boring, unpleasant, or tedious, we may put it off in favor of more enjoyable activities.

2. **Ambiguity:** Unclear instructions or ambiguous goals can contribute to procrastination. When we're uncertain about what is expected of us or how to approach a task, we may delay taking action until we have more clarity.

3. **Lack of Structure:** Without clear deadlines or a structured plan in place, it's easy to procrastinate. When there's no sense of urgency or accountability, we may struggle to prioritize tasks and manage our time effectively.

4. **Environmental Distractions:** External distractions, such as noise, technology, or interruptions, can derail our focus and lead to procrastination. When our environment is conducive to procrastination, it becomes even harder to stay on task.

5. **Reward Sensitivity:** Some individuals are more sensitive to immediate rewards and are therefore more likely to procrastinate on tasks with delayed gratification. They may prioritize short-term pleasure over long-term goals, leading to procrastination.

Types of Procrastinators

Procrastination manifests in different ways, and researchers have identified several distinct types of procrastinators based on underlying motivations and behaviors.

1. **The Perfectionist:** Perfectionists strive for flawlessness and may procrastinate out of fear of making mistakes or

falling short of their high standards. They often delay starting a task until they feel confident they can achieve perfection.

2. **The Avoider:** Avoiders procrastinate to escape feelings of discomfort or anxiety associated with a task. They may engage in avoidance behaviors, such as distraction or denial, to avoid confronting the task at hand.

3. **The Thrill-Seeker:** Thrill-seekers thrive on the adrenaline rush of working under pressure and may intentionally procrastinate to create a sense of urgency. They may wait until the last minute to start a task, believing they perform best under pressure.

4. **The Indecisive:** Indecisive procrastinators struggle with decision-making and may delay starting a task due to uncertainty or indecision. They may agonize over choices, second-guessing themselves and ultimately procrastinating on taking action.

5. **The Overwhelmed:** Overwhelmed procrastinators feel paralyzed by the sheer magnitude of tasks facing them. They may procrastinate as a coping mechanism, avoiding the overwhelming feelings of stress and anxiety associated with tackling their to-do list.

6. **The Habitual Procrastinator:** Habitual procrastinators have developed a pattern of delaying tasks consistently over time. Procrastination has become a habitual behavior, ingrained in their daily routines and difficult to break.

The Procrastination-Perfectionism Connection

Procrastination and perfectionism are closely intertwined, often feeding off each other in a vicious cycle. Perfectionists may procrastinate out of fear of not meeting their own impossibly high standards, while procrastinators may adopt perfectionistic tendencies as a way to justify their avoidance behavior.

Perfectionism can manifest in different forms, including:

1. **Self-Oriented Perfectionism:** Setting unrealistic standards for oneself and striving for perfection at all costs.

2. **Others-Oriented Perfectionism:** Imposing high standards on others and expecting perfection from those around us.

3. **Socially Prescribed Perfectionism:** Feeling pressure from external sources, such as family, peers, or society, to meet unrealistic standards of perfection.

Perfectionists may procrastinate because they fear failure or criticism, believing that anything less than perfect is unacceptable. They may also delay starting a task until they feel confident they can achieve perfection, leading to chronic procrastination and increased stress.

Understanding the connection between procrastination and perfectionism is essential for developing effective strategies for managing both. By challenging perfectionistic beliefs and adopting a more flexible, self-compassionate mindset, we can break free from the cycle of procrastination and perfectionism and cultivate healthier, more productive habits.

In the next chapter, we'll explore the consequences of procrastination and the impact it can have on various aspects of our lives. From academic and professional performance to emotional well-being and relationships, procrastination's effects are far-reaching and profound. But by understanding these consequences, we can begin to take proactive steps toward change and growth.

CHAPTER THREE
CONSEQUENCES OF PROCRASTINATION
Focus: Examining the Impact

In the previous chapters, we delved into the psychology of procrastination, uncovering its roots and exploring the various types of procrastinators. Now, let's turn our attention to the consequences of procrastination. What happens when we put off important tasks, delay taking action, and let deadlines slip by? From academic and professional performance to emotional well-being and relationships, the effects of procrastination can be far-reaching and profound.

Emotional Impact

Procrastination often takes a toll on our emotional well-being, leading to feelings of stress, anxiety, guilt, and frustration. When we procrastinate, we experience a constant underlying sense of unease, knowing that there's a looming deadline or unfinished task hanging over our heads. This chronic stress can have detrimental effects on both our mental and physical health.

1. **Stress:** Procrastination is a major source of stress for many people. The longer we put off a task, the more pressure we feel to complete it, leading to heightened levels of stress and anxiety. This constant state of tension can negatively impact our mood, sleep, and overall quality of life.

2. **Anxiety:** Procrastination is often driven by underlying feelings of anxiety or fear. We may worry about not meeting expectations, making mistakes, or facing criticism from others. These fears can intensify as deadlines approach, exacerbating our anxiety and making it even harder to start or complete tasks.

3. **Guilt:** Procrastination is accompanied by a pervasive sense of guilt, knowing that we're not living up to our own expectations or fulfilling our responsibilities. We may feel guilty for wasting time, letting others down, or failing to meet deadlines. This guilt can further erode our self-esteem and motivation.

4. **Frustration:** Procrastination can lead to feelings of frustration and self-criticism. We may berate ourselves for our perceived laziness or lack of discipline, further fueling the cycle of procrastination. This frustration can escalate over time, making it even harder to break free from procrastination habits.

Academic and Professional Consequences

Procrastination can have serious repercussions on our academic and professional performance, affecting our grades, job performance, and career prospects. When we put off important tasks, we may struggle to meet deadlines, produce subpar work, and miss out on valuable opportunities for growth and advancement.

1. **Missed Deadlines:** Procrastination often results in missed deadlines, leading to late submissions, incomplete assignments, and lower grades. This can have significant consequences for students, impacting their academic standing and future opportunities.

2. **Poor Performance:** Procrastination can also affect the quality of our work. When we rush to complete tasks at the last minute, we may produce work that is sloppy, incomplete, or riddled with errors. This can undermine our credibility and professionalism in the workplace.

3. **Career Stagnation:** In the professional realm, procrastination can hinder career advancement and growth. When we consistently fail to meet deadlines or deliver results, we may be passed over for promotions, raises, or important projects. This can stall our career progression and limit our opportunities for success.

4. **Increased Stress:** The pressure of impending deadlines and the consequences of procrastination can contribute to elevated levels of stress in both academic and professional settings. This chronic stress can lead to burnout, decreased job satisfaction, and even health problems.

Relationship Effects

Procrastination can also impact our relationships with others, affecting our ability to communicate effectively, collaborate productively, and maintain trust and respect. When we procrastinate, we may let down friends, family members, or colleagues, leading to feelings of frustration, resentment, and disappointment.

1. **Missed Opportunities:** Procrastination can result in missed opportunities to connect with others and strengthen relationships. When we prioritize tasks over spending time with loved ones or fulfilling commitments, we may strain our relationships and miss out on meaningful experiences.

2. **Broken Trust:** Procrastination can erode trust in relationships, particularly when others rely on us to follow through on our promises or commitments. When we consistently fail to deliver or meet expectations, we may damage the trust and credibility we've built with others.

3. **Communication Breakdown:** Procrastination can lead to breakdowns in communication, as delayed responses or incomplete tasks can cause misunderstandings and frustration. Effective communication is essential for healthy relationships, and procrastination can undermine this critical aspect of interpersonal dynamics.

4. **Resentment:** Procrastination can breed feelings of resentment in relationships, as others may feel taken advantage of or burdened by our procrastination habits. Resentment can poison the atmosphere of a relationship, leading to conflict and emotional distance.

Coping Mechanisms

While the consequences of procrastination can be significant, it's essential to remember that it's never too late to change course. By adopting healthier habits, improving time management skills, and addressing underlying issues such as perfectionism or fear of failure, we can begin to overcome procrastination and mitigate its negative effects.

1. **Setting Realistic Goals:** Break tasks down into smaller, more manageable goals and set realistic deadlines for completing them. This can help alleviate feelings of overwhelm and make tasks seem more achievable.

2. **Prioritizing Tasks:** Identify the most important tasks and prioritize them based on urgency and importance. Focus on completing high-priority tasks first, and allocate time and resources accordingly.

3. **Creating Accountability:** Hold yourself accountable for your actions by sharing your goals and progress with others. This can provide motivation and encouragement, as well as accountability to follow through on your commitments.

4. **Seeking Support:** Reach out to friends, family members, or colleagues for support and encouragement. Surround yourself with positive influences who can help keep you motivated and on track.

5. **Practicing Self-Compassion:** Be gentle with yourself and practice self-compassion when you slip up or make mistakes. Acknowledge your efforts and progress, and recognize that change takes time and effort.

In the next chapter, we'll explore strategies for recognizing and overcoming procrastination patterns, empowering you to take control of your habits and achieve your goals with greater ease and efficiency. By understanding the consequences of procrastination and implementing proactive coping mechanisms, you can begin to break free from the cycle of procrastination and cultivate a more fulfilling and productive life.

CHAPTER FOUR
RECOGNIZING PROCRASTINATION PATTERNS
Focus: Triggers, Excuses, and Exercises

In the journey to overcome procrastination, one of the crucial steps is recognizing the patterns and behaviors that contribute to this habit. Procrastination often operates subtly, disguising itself as temporary distractions or legitimate reasons for delaying tasks. However, by developing self-awareness and identifying the triggers and excuses that lead to procrastination, we can begin to take proactive steps towards breaking free from its grip.

Identifying Your Procrastination Triggers

Procrastination triggers are the situations, emotions, or thoughts that prompt us to put off tasks or delay taking action. These triggers can vary widely from person to person and may be influenced by factors such as personality, environment, and past experiences. By recognizing our individual triggers, we can learn to anticipate and address them more effectively.

1. **Fear of Failure:** Fear of failure is a common trigger for procrastination. When we doubt our abilities or worry about not meeting expectations, we may avoid starting a task altogether to protect ourselves from the possibility of failure. Recognizing when fear of failure is driving our procrastination can help us confront these fears and move forward with greater confidence.

2. **Perfectionism:** Perfectionism is another significant trigger for procrastination. When we set impossibly high standards for ourselves and fear that anything less than perfect will be deemed a failure, we may delay starting a task until we feel confident we can achieve perfection. By acknowledging our perfectionistic tendencies, we can work towards adopting a more flexible and realistic approach to goal-setting and task completion.

3. **Overwhelm:** Feeling overwhelmed by the sheer magnitude of tasks facing us can also trigger procrastination. When we're confronted with a long to-do list or complex project, we may struggle to know where to start and end up avoiding the task altogether. Breaking tasks down into smaller, more manageable steps can help alleviate feelings of overwhelm and make it easier to get started.

4. **Lack of Motivation:** A lack of motivation can be a powerful trigger for procrastination. When we don't feel inspired or passionate about a task, we may struggle to muster the energy and enthusiasm needed to get started. Recognizing when our motivation is flagging can help us explore ways to reignite our passion and find meaning in our work.

5. **Distractions:** External distractions, such as social media, television, or household chores, can also trigger procrastination. When we're faced with tempting distractions, we may find it difficult to focus on the task at hand and end up procrastinating instead. Identifying our

most common distractions and finding ways to minimize or eliminate them can help us stay focused and productive.

Common Procrastination Excuses

Procrastination often goes hand in hand with a repertoire of excuses that we use to justify our avoidance behavior. These excuses can range from seemingly legitimate reasons to thinly veiled attempts to rationalize our procrastination. By becoming aware of the excuses we make and challenging them head-on, we can begin to dismantle the barriers that keep us stuck in procrastination mode.

1. **"I'll Do It Later":** The classic procrastinator's mantra, "I'll do it later," is perhaps the most common excuse for putting off tasks. While it may seem harmless in the moment, this mentality can quickly snowball into a pattern of chronic procrastination. By recognizing when we're falling into the trap of delaying tasks unnecessarily, we can take steps to break the cycle and tackle tasks head-on.

2. **"I Work Best Under Pressure":** Some people use the excuse that they work best under pressure as a justification for procrastination. While it's true that some individuals thrive on the adrenaline rush of a looming deadline, relying on last-minute pressure can lead to increased stress, lower-quality work, and missed opportunities for planning and preparation.

3. **"I Don't Have Enough Time":** Another common excuse for procrastination is a lack of time. We may convince

ourselves that we're too busy to start a task or that we'll have more time to complete it later. However, this excuse often masks deeper issues such as poor time management skills or a lack of prioritization. By learning to manage our time more effectively and prioritize tasks, we can make better use of the time we have available.

4. **"I'm Not in the Right Mood":** Some people use their mood as an excuse for procrastination, waiting until they feel motivated or inspired to start a task. However, waiting for the perfect mood or mindset can be a recipe for procrastination, as moods are often transient and unpredictable. By adopting a proactive approach to task initiation and focusing on action rather than mood, we can overcome this excuse and make progress even when we don't feel like it.

5. **"It's Not Important":** We may also procrastinate on tasks by convincing ourselves that they're not important or urgent. While it's true that some tasks may be lower priority than others, procrastinating on important tasks can have serious consequences for our academic, professional, and personal lives. By recognizing the importance of completing tasks in a timely manner, we can overcome this excuse and prioritize our responsibilities accordingly.

Self-Reflection Exercises

Self-reflection is a powerful tool for recognizing procrastination patterns and challenging the excuses that keep us stuck. By taking the time to examine our thoughts, feelings, and behaviors related to procrastination, we can gain valuable insights into our habits and motivations. The following self-reflection exercises can help us develop greater self-awareness and identify opportunities for growth and change.

1. **Journaling:** Set aside time each day to journal about your experiences with procrastination. Reflect on the tasks you've been avoiding, the excuses you've been making, and the emotions underlying your procrastination. Writing can help clarify your thoughts and feelings, making it easier to identify patterns and triggers.

2. **Mindfulness Practice:** Incorporate mindfulness practices into your daily routine to cultivate greater awareness of your thoughts and emotions. Mindfulness techniques such as meditation, deep breathing, and body scanning can help you tune into your internal experiences and recognize when procrastination patterns are emerging.

3. **Behavior Tracking:** Keep track of your procrastination behaviors using a journal or smartphone app. Record the tasks you've been putting off, the excuses you've been making, and the specific triggers that led to procrastination. Analyzing this data over time can help you identify patterns and develop strategies for overcoming procrastination.

4. **Goal Setting:** Set specific, achievable goals for overcoming procrastination and improving productivity. Break larger goals down into smaller, more manageable steps, and create a plan for tackling them systematically.

Setting deadlines and accountability measures can help keep you motivated and on track.

5. **Seeking Feedback:** Ask friends, family members, or colleagues for feedback on your procrastination habits. They may be able to offer valuable insights and perspectives that you hadn't considered. Be open to constructive criticism and use it as an opportunity for growth and self-improvement.

Conclusion

Recognizing procrastination patterns and challenging the excuses that contribute to them is a crucial step on the path to overcoming procrastination. By developing self-awareness, identifying triggers, and practicing self-reflection, we can begin to dismantle the barriers that keep us stuck in procrastination mode.

In the next chapter, we'll explore practical strategies for overcoming procrastination and cultivating healthier habits that promote productivity and success.

CHAPTER FIVE
OVERCOMING FEAR OF FAILURE
Focus: Understanding, Embracing, and Growing

Fear of failure is a pervasive and powerful force that often underlies procrastination. It's the nagging voice in our heads that tells us we're not good enough, that our efforts will fall short, and that we're better off not trying at all. But the truth is, failure is an inevitable part of the human experience, and avoiding it at all costs only serves to hold us back from reaching our full potential. In this chapter, we'll explore strategies for overcoming fear of failure and embracing imperfection as essential steps on the journey to overcoming procrastination.

Understanding Fear of Failure

Fear of failure is a universal human experience, stemming from a deep-seated desire to avoid negative outcomes and preserve our self-esteem. It's a natural response to uncertainty and risk, rooted in our evolutionary instincts to protect ourselves from harm. However, when fear of failure becomes excessive or irrational, it can paralyze us and prevent us from taking the necessary risks to achieve our goals.

1. **Perfectionism:** Perfectionists are particularly prone to fear of failure, as they hold themselves to impossibly high standards and fear that anything less than perfect will be deemed a failure. They may avoid starting tasks altogether

or procrastinate indefinitely in a misguided attempt to avoid making mistakes.

2. **Self-Doubt:** Individuals with low self-esteem or self-confidence may also struggle with fear of failure, doubting their abilities and worrying about not measuring up to others' expectations. They may engage in negative self-talk and undermine their own confidence, making it even harder to overcome procrastination and take action.

3. **Imposter Syndrome:** Imposter syndrome is a psychological phenomenon characterized by feelings of inadequacy and self-doubt, despite evidence of success and competence. People with imposter syndrome may fear being exposed as a fraud or worry that they don't deserve their achievements, leading to procrastination and avoidance behavior.

Embracing Imperfection

Contrary to popular belief, perfection is not attainable, nor is it desirable. The pursuit of perfection often leads to frustration, anxiety, and paralysis, preventing us from making progress and enjoying the process of learning and growth. Embracing imperfection is essential for overcoming procrastination and cultivating a mindset of resilience and self-compassion.

1. **Redefining Success:** Instead of striving for perfection, redefine success as progress, effort, and resilience. Recognize that failure is a natural part of the learning process and an opportunity for growth and improvement.

Celebrate your efforts and accomplishments, no matter how small, and focus on continuous improvement rather than unattainable ideals.

2. **Cultivating Self-Compassion:** Practice self-compassion by treating yourself with kindness and understanding, especially in the face of failure or setbacks. Acknowledge your efforts and progress, and remind yourself that everyone makes mistakes and experiences failure at some point. Treat yourself with the same empathy and compassion you would offer to a friend facing similar challenges.

3. **Setting Realistic Expectations:** Adjust your expectations to align with reality, recognizing that perfection is neither necessary nor achievable. Set realistic, achievable goals for yourself, and break larger tasks down into smaller, more manageable steps. Focus on making progress rather than achieving perfection, and celebrate your accomplishments along the way.

4. **Learning from Mistakes:** Instead of viewing failure as a reflection of your worth or abilities, see it as an opportunity for learning and growth. Analyze your mistakes objectively, identify what went wrong, and brainstorm ways to improve in the future. Every failure is a valuable lesson that brings you one step closer to success.

Cultivating a Growth Mindset

At the heart of overcoming fear of failure and embracing imperfection is the concept of a growth mindset. A growth mindset is the belief that our abilities and intelligence can be developed through effort, practice, and perseverance. It's the antidote to a fixed mindset, which assumes that our talents and capabilities are static and unchangeable.

1. **Embracing Challenges:** Embrace challenges as opportunities for growth and learning, rather than obstacles to be avoided. View setbacks and failures as natural parts of the learning process and opportunities to stretch beyond your comfort zone.

2. **Persisting in the Face of Adversity:** Develop resilience and perseverance by persisting in the face of adversity. When faced with setbacks or obstacles, remind yourself that setbacks are temporary and that success often requires perseverance and resilience.

3. **Seeking Feedback:** Seek out constructive feedback from others as a way to learn and grow. Welcome criticism as an opportunity to identify areas for improvement and refine your skills. Be open to feedback, even if it's difficult to hear, and use it as a catalyst for growth and self-improvement.

4. **Inspiring Others:** Inspire others with your growth mindset by leading by example and demonstrating resilience, perseverance, and a willingness to learn. Share your experiences and lessons learned with others, and encourage them to adopt a growth mindset of their own.

Practical Strategies for Overcoming Fear of Failure

In addition to cultivating a growth mindset and embracing imperfection, there are several practical strategies you can use to overcome fear of failure and reduce procrastination.

1. **Visualizing Success:** Visualize yourself succeeding in your goals and overcoming obstacles, using vivid imagery and positive affirmations to reinforce your confidence and motivation.

2. **Taking Incremental Steps:** Break tasks down into smaller, more manageable steps, and focus on completing one step at a time. This can help reduce feelings of overwhelm and make it easier to get started.

3. **Setting Process Goals:** Instead of focusing solely on outcomes, set process goals that emphasize the effort and progress you make along the way. Celebrate your efforts and accomplishments, regardless of the outcome.

4. **Practicing Self-Reflection:** Regularly reflect on your thoughts, feelings, and behaviors related to fear of failure and procrastination. Identify patterns and triggers, and develop strategies for challenging negative beliefs and self-limiting thoughts.

5. **Seeking Support:** Reach out to friends, family members, or a therapist for support and encouragement. Surround yourself with positive influences who believe in

your ability to succeed and are willing to support you on your journey.

Conclusion

Overcoming fear of failure and embracing imperfection are essential steps on the journey to overcoming procrastination and achieving our goals. By cultivating a growth mindset, practicing self-compassion, and setting realistic expectations, we can break free from the paralysis of perfectionism and take proactive steps towards success.

In the next chapter, we'll explore strategies for setting realistic goals, managing time effectively, and overcoming procrastination habits that hold us back from reaching our full potential. Through intentional action and a commitment to growth, we can transform fear into fuel and embrace imperfection as the key to unlocking our full potential and achieving our goals with greater ease and confidence.

CHAPTER SIX
BREAKING THE PERFECTIONISM CYCLE
Focus: Changing Your Mindset

Perfectionism, often intertwined with procrastination, can be a significant barrier to productivity and personal fulfillment. In this chapter, we'll explore how to break free from the perfectionism cycle by challenging all-or-nothing thinking, practicing self-compassion, and learning from mistakes.

Understanding the Perfectionism Trap

Perfectionism is a double-edged sword. On one hand, it can drive us to excel and strive for excellence in our endeavors. On the other hand, it can paralyze us with fear of failure and prevent us from taking action. Understanding the perfectionism trap is the first step towards breaking free from its grip.

Recognizing All-or-Nothing Thinking

Perfectionists tend to see the world in black and white, viewing any outcome that falls short of perfection as a failure. This all-or-nothing thinking can lead to unrealistic expectations, excessive self-criticism, and chronic procrastination. By recognizing when we're engaging in this cognitive distortion, we can begin to challenge its hold on us.

Reframing Failure as Feedback

Instead of viewing setbacks and mistakes as evidence of our inadequacy, we can reframe them as opportunities for growth and learning. Failure is not a reflection of our worth as individuals but rather a natural part of the learning process. Embracing failure as feedback allows us to extract valuable lessons and use them to inform our future actions and decisions.

Setting Realistic Expectations

Perfectionists often set impossibly high standards for themselves, leading to constant frustration and dissatisfaction. To break free from this cycle, we must set realistic and achievable goals that allow for mistakes and setbacks along the way. Recognizing that progress, not perfection, is the ultimate measure of success can help us shift our focus from unattainable ideals to meaningful progress.

Cultivating Self-Compassion

Self-compassion is the antidote to the harsh self-criticism and unrealistic expectations that plague perfectionists. By treating ourselves with kindness and understanding, we can cultivate resilience, self-acceptance, and a greater sense of well-being.

Practicing Self-Kindness

Treating ourselves with kindness and compassion begins with the recognition that we are human beings, flawed and imperfect, yet deserving of love and acceptance. Instead of berating ourselves for mistakes or shortcomings, we can offer words of encouragement and support, just as we would to a friend in need.

Embracing Imperfection

Perfectionism thrives on the belief that anything less than perfect is unacceptable. By embracing our imperfections as unique aspects of our identity, we can challenge this belief and cultivate a greater sense of self-acceptance. Recognizing that true beauty lies in our authenticity allows us to let go of the relentless pursuit of perfection and embrace the messy, imperfect journey of self-discovery.

Letting Go of Comparison

Comparing ourselves to others is a surefire way to undermine our self-worth and fuel feelings of inadequacy. Instead of measuring our success against someone else's, we can focus on our own progress and growth. Celebrating our achievements, no matter how small, and recognizing that everyone's journey is unique can help us break free from the comparison trap and cultivate greater self-compassion.

Learning from Mistakes

Mistakes are an inevitable part of the human experience, yet many perfectionists see them as unacceptable failures. By reframing mistakes as valuable learning opportunities, we can extract meaning and growth from even the most challenging experiences.

Embracing a Growth Mindset

Instead of viewing challenges as threats to our competence, we can see them as opportunities to stretch beyond our comfort zone and expand our capabilities. Embracing a growth mindset allows us to approach failure with curiosity and openness, eager to learn and grow from our experiences.

Analyzing Failure Objectively

When faced with failure or setbacks, it can be tempting to blame ourselves or dwell on negative emotions. However, approaching the situation with curiosity and openness allows us to analyze failure objectively, seeking to understand what went wrong and how we can improve in the future. Using failure as a diagnostic tool empowers us to identify areas for growth and development, transforming setbacks into opportunities for progress.

Celebrating Progress, Not Perfection

Shifting our focus from achieving perfection to making progress is a powerful antidote to the perfectionism trap.

By celebrating small victories along the way, we recognize the value of our efforts and stay motivated to continue moving forward. Embracing progress over perfection allows us to cultivate a greater sense of fulfillment and joy in our journey towards personal and professional growth.

Conclusion

Breaking free from the perfectionism cycle is a transformative journey that requires courage, self-awareness, and compassion. By challenging all-or-nothing thinking, practicing self-compassion, and learning from mistakes, we can overcome the barriers that hold us back and embrace a more fulfilling and authentic way of living.

In the next chapter, we'll explore practical strategies for managing our time effectively and overcoming procrastination habits that hinder our progress. Through intentional action and self-reflection, we can cultivate a mindset of resilience and self-acceptance that empowers us to thrive in all areas of our lives.

CHAPTER SEVEN
TIME-MANAGEMENT STRATEGIES
Focus: Prioritize To Be Effective

Effective time management is essential for overcoming procrastination and maximizing productivity. In this chapter, we'll explore practical strategies for managing your time effectively and overcoming procrastination habits that hinder your progress.

Understanding the Importance of Time Management

Time is a finite resource, and how we choose to allocate it can have a profound impact on our lives. Effective time management allows us to prioritize tasks, minimize distractions, and make the most of our precious time. By mastering the art of time management, we can increase our productivity, reduce stress, and achieve our goals with greater ease and efficiency.

The Cost of Procrastination

Procrastination comes with a steep cost. When we put off important tasks until the last minute, we rob ourselves of the opportunity to do our best work and achieve our full potential. Procrastination can lead to missed deadlines, increased stress, and a sense of guilt and regret. By managing our time effectively, we can break free from the cycle of procrastination and take control of our lives.

The Benefits of Effective Time Management

On the other hand, effective time management brings a host of benefits. By setting priorities, creating a schedule, and sticking to deadlines, we can increase our productivity and accomplish more in less time. Time management allows us to focus our energy on the tasks that matter most, leading to greater satisfaction and success in all areas of our lives.

Prioritization Techniques

Prioritization is the foundation of effective time management. By identifying the most important tasks and focusing our efforts on them, we can maximize our productivity and make steady progress towards our goals. Here are some practical techniques for prioritizing tasks:

The Eisenhower Matrix

The Eisenhower Matrix, also known as the Urgent-Important Matrix, is a powerful tool for prioritizing tasks based on their urgency and importance. Divide your tasks into four quadrants:

- Quadrant 1: Urgent and Important - tasks that require immediate attention
- Quadrant 2: Important but Not Urgent - tasks that contribute to long-term goals and priorities
- Quadrant 3: Urgent but Not Important - tasks that can be delegated or eliminated

- Quadrant 4: Neither Urgent nor Important - tasks that are low priority and can be postponed or eliminated

Focus on completing tasks in Quadrant 1 and Quadrant 2, as these are the tasks that have the greatest impact on your goals and priorities.

The ABCDE Method

The ABCDE Method is another effective technique for prioritizing tasks. Assign each task a letter from A to E based on its importance:

- A tasks are the most important and must be completed today
- B tasks are important but can be completed at a later date
- C tasks are nice to do but not essential
- D tasks can be delegated to someone else
- E tasks can be eliminated altogether

Focus on completing your A tasks first, then move on to your B tasks, and so on. This method helps you focus your time and energy on the tasks that will have the greatest impact on your goals.

Creating Effective To-Do Lists

To-do lists are a simple yet powerful tool for managing your time and staying organized. By breaking down your tasks into manageable chunks and prioritizing them, you can ensure that nothing falls through the cracks. Here are some tips for creating effective to-do lists:

Keep It Simple

Keep your to-do list simple and focused. Limit the number of tasks you include to avoid feeling overwhelmed, and prioritize them based on their importance. Focus on the most important tasks that will move you closer to your goals.

Break Tasks into Smaller Steps

Break larger tasks down into smaller, more manageable steps. This makes them less intimidating and easier to tackle, increasing your motivation and momentum. Instead of putting "write report" on your to-do list, break it down into smaller steps like "research topic," "outline report," and "write first draft."

Use Time Estimates

Estimate how long each task will take to complete and allocate time accordingly. This helps you budget your time more effectively and prevents you from overcommitting yourself. Be realistic in your estimates and allow extra time for unexpected delays or interruptions.

Utilizing Time-Blocking Methods

Time-blocking is a time management technique that involves scheduling specific blocks of time for different tasks and activities. By allocating time to specific tasks and protecting that time from interruptions, you can increase your focus and productivity. Here's how to use time-blocking effectively:

Identify Your Most Productive Hours

Identify your most productive hours, when you're alert, focused, and energized. Schedule your most important tasks during these times to maximize your productivity and make the most of your peak performance periods.

Allocate Time for Important Tasks

Block out time in your schedule for important tasks and activities, such as work projects, exercise, and self-care. Prioritize these blocks of time and protect them from distractions and interruptions to ensure that you can focus fully on the task at hand.

Schedule Breaks and Downtime

In addition to scheduling time for work and productivity, don't forget to schedule breaks and downtime to rest and recharge. Taking regular breaks helps prevent burnout and improves overall productivity and well-being. Include short breaks throughout your day and schedule longer breaks for meals, exercise, and relaxation.

Conclusion

Effective time management is a key ingredient in overcoming procrastination and achieving success in all areas of life. By prioritizing tasks, creating effective to-do lists, and utilizing time-blocking methods, we can maximize our productivity and make steady progress towards our goals.

In the next chapter, we'll explore proactive strategies for overcoming procrastination and staying on track even when faced with distractions and challenges. Through intentional action and a commitment to effective time management, we can take control of our time and create the life we desire.

CHAPTER EIGHT
OVERCOMING PROCRASTINATION PROACTIVELY
Focus: Strategies to Stay On Track

Procrastination is a common challenge that many people face, often leading to feelings of frustration, guilt, and stress. In this chapter, we'll explore proactive strategies for overcoming procrastination and staying on track towards our goals, even when faced with distractions and challenges.

Understanding the Root Causes of Procrastination

Before we can effectively overcome procrastination, it's important to understand its underlying causes. Procrastination can stem from a variety of factors, including fear of failure, perfectionism, lack of motivation, and poor time management skills. By identifying the root causes of our procrastination tendencies, we can develop targeted strategies to address them.

Fear of Failure

One of the most common reasons people procrastinate is fear of failure. When we're afraid of falling short of our own or others' expectations, we may avoid taking action altogether. This fear can be paralyzing, preventing us from pursuing our goals and dreams. By recognizing that failure is a natural part of the learning process and reframing it as an opportunity for growth, we can overcome this fear and take proactive steps towards success.

Perfectionism

Perfectionism is another common cause of procrastination. When we set impossibly high standards for ourselves and our work, we may feel overwhelmed and anxious, leading us to procrastinate rather than risk falling short of perfection. By embracing a mindset of progress over perfection and celebrating our efforts, we can break free from the perfectionism trap and move forward with confidence.

Lack of Motivation

Sometimes, procrastination stems from a lack of motivation or interest in the task at hand. When we don't feel excited or engaged by what we're doing, it's easy to put it off in favor of more enjoyable activities. Finding ways to increase our motivation, such as setting meaningful goals, breaking tasks into smaller steps, and creating a supportive environment, can help us overcome procrastination and stay focused on our objectives.

Poor Time Management Skills

Finally, poor time management skills can contribute to procrastination by making it difficult to prioritize tasks and allocate time effectively. When we're unsure of how to manage our time, we may feel overwhelmed by the sheer volume of work ahead of us and resort to procrastination as a coping mechanism. By learning and implementing effective time management strategies, we can regain control of our schedules and make steady progress towards our goals.

Setting Deadlines and Accountability

One of the most effective ways to overcome procrastination is to set deadlines for ourselves and hold ourselves accountable for meeting them. Deadlines create a sense of urgency and provide a clear target to work towards, motivating us to take action and make progress on our goals. Here are some tips for setting deadlines and holding yourself accountable:

Break Tasks into Smaller Steps

Breaking larger tasks down into smaller, more manageable steps can make them less intimidating and easier to tackle. Set deadlines for each step along the way, and track your progress as you work towards completing the task. This incremental approach helps prevent procrastination by providing a clear roadmap to follow.

Use SMART Goals

SMART goals are specific, measurable, achievable, relevant, and time-bound. By setting SMART goals for yourself, you can ensure that your objectives are clear, attainable, and aligned with your priorities. Write down your goals and deadlines, and review them regularly to stay focused and motivated.

Find an Accountability Partner

Having an accountability partner can be a powerful motivator for overcoming procrastination. Choose someone you trust and respect, and share your goals and deadlines with them. Check in regularly to update them on your progress and seek support and encouragement when needed. Knowing that someone else is counting on you can provide the extra motivation you need to stay on track.

Breaking Tasks into Smaller Steps

As mentioned earlier, breaking larger tasks down into smaller, more manageable steps is an effective strategy for overcoming procrastination. This approach helps prevent overwhelm and makes it easier to get started on the task at hand. Here's how to break tasks into smaller steps:

Identify the Next Action

Begin by identifying the next action you need to take to move forward on the task. This could be something as simple as making a phone call, sending an email, or gathering information. By focusing on the next actionable step, you can overcome inertia and build momentum towards completing the task.

Set a Timer

Set a timer for a short period of time, such as 25 minutes, and commit to working on the task uninterrupted until the timer goes off. This technique, known as the Pomodoro Technique, helps break tasks into manageable chunks and prevents procrastination by creating a sense of urgency and focus.

Reward Yourself

Reward yourself for completing each small step along the way. This could be something as simple as taking a short break, enjoying a cup of coffee, or treating yourself to a favorite snack. By associating progress with positive reinforcement, you can increase your motivation and reduce the likelihood of procrastination.

Utilizing the Pomodoro Technique

The Pomodoro Technique is a time management method that involves breaking work into intervals of focused work followed by short breaks. Here's how to use the Pomodoro Technique effectively:

Choose a Task to Focus On

Start by choosing a task to work on and setting a timer for 25 minutes. During this time, focus exclusively on the task at hand, avoiding distractions and interruptions as much as possible.

Work Intensely for 25 Minutes

During the 25-minute work interval, work as intensely and efficiently as possible. Avoid multitasking and stay focused on the task until the timer goes off.

Take a Short Break

After 25 minutes of focused work, take a short break lasting 5 minutes. Use this time to relax, stretch, or recharge before starting the next work interval.

Repeat the Process

Continue alternating between 25-minute work intervals and 5-minute breaks until you've completed four cycles, then take a longer break lasting 15-30 minutes. This cycle of focused work and short breaks helps maintain motivation and prevent burnout, making it easier to overcome procrastination and stay productive throughout the day.

Conclusion

Overcoming procrastination requires proactive effort and a willingness to confront the underlying causes of our procrastination tendencies. By setting deadlines and holding ourselves accountable, breaking tasks into smaller steps, and utilizing strategies like the Pomodoro Technique, we can overcome procrastination and make steady progress towards our goals.

In the next chapter, we'll explore the importance of building motivation and momentum to maintain productivity and stay on track even when faced with challenges and distractions. Through intentional action and a commitment to proactive strategies, we can overcome procrastination and achieve success in all areas of our lives.

CHAPTER NINE
BUILDING MOTIVATION AND MOMENTUM
Focus: Be Productive and Proactive

Motivation is the fuel that drives us towards our goals, while momentum keeps us moving forward even when faced with obstacles and challenges. In this chapter, we'll explore the importance of building motivation and momentum to maintain productivity and stay on track towards our objectives.

Understanding Motivation

Motivation is the internal drive that compels us to take action towards our goals. It is the force that propels us out of bed in the morning, fuels our efforts, and sustains us through challenges and setbacks. Without motivation, even the most well-laid plans can fall by the wayside. Understanding what motivates us and how to cultivate and maintain motivation is essential for achieving success in any endeavor.

Intrinsic vs. Extrinsic Motivation

Motivation can be broadly categorized into two types: intrinsic and extrinsic. Intrinsic motivation comes from within and is driven by personal values, interests, and passions. It is the desire to engage in an activity for its own sake, simply because it is enjoyable or meaningful. Extrinsic motivation, on the other hand, comes from external rewards or pressures, such as money, recognition, or social approval. While extrinsic motivation can be effective in the short term, it is often less sustainable and fulfilling than intrinsic motivation.

Finding Your Why

At the heart of motivation lies a sense of purpose or "why" – the reason behind our actions and goals. Understanding why a goal is important to us and how it aligns with our values and aspirations can provide the motivation and clarity needed to stay committed and focused, even when faced with challenges. Take the time to reflect on your goals and ask yourself why they matter to you. What impact do you hope to have? What values are you striving to uphold? By connecting your goals to a deeper sense of purpose, you can tap into a powerful source of motivation that will sustain you through adversity.

Setting Meaningful Goals

Meaningful goals are those that resonate with our values, interests, and aspirations. They are goals that inspire us, challenge us, and align with our vision for the future. When setting goals, it's important to consider not only what we want to achieve but also why it matters to us personally. By setting goals that are meaningful and relevant to our lives, we can increase our motivation and commitment to achieving them.

Creating a Vision Board

A vision board is a visual representation of your goals, dreams, and aspirations. It can be a powerful tool for building motivation and momentum by providing a tangible reminder of what you're working towards and why it matters to you. Here's how to create a vision board:

Gather Materials

Start by gathering materials for your vision board, such as poster board, magazines, newspapers, scissors, glue, and markers. Choose images, words, and phrases that resonate with your goals and aspirations.

Visualize Your Goals

Take some time to visualize your goals and dreams in vivid detail. What do you want to achieve? How will it feel to accomplish your goals? Use this visualization as inspiration for selecting images and words for your vision board.

Arrange and Glue

Arrange your chosen images, words, and phrases on the poster board in a way that feels meaningful and inspiring to you. Get creative and experiment with different layouts and designs until you find one that resonates with your vision.

Display Your Vision Board

Once you've finished creating your vision board, display it in a prominent place where you'll see it every day, such as your bedroom or office. Take a few moments each day to look at your vision board and visualize yourself achieving your goals. Allow it to inspire and motivate you to take action towards your dreams.

Creating a Reward System

Rewarding yourself for reaching milestones and achieving goals is an effective way to build motivation and momentum. By celebrating your progress and acknowledging your accomplishments, you can reinforce positive behaviors and stay motivated to continue moving forward. Here's how to create a reward system:

Set Clear Milestones

Break your goals down into smaller milestones or checkpoints, and set clear criteria for what constitutes success at each stage. This could be completing a certain number of tasks, reaching a specific milestone, or achieving a predetermined level of progress.

Choose Meaningful Rewards

Choose rewards that are meaningful and motivating to you personally. They could be something as simple as treating yourself to a favorite meal or activity, or something more substantial like a weekend getaway or a new piece of equipment or technology.

Track Your Progress

Keep track of your progress towards your goals and milestones, and celebrate each achievement along the way. This could be as simple as checking off items on a checklist or using a visual progress tracker to see how far you've come.

Celebrate Your Successes

When you reach a milestone or achieve a goal, take the time to celebrate your success and reward yourself for your hard work and dedication. Acknowledge your accomplishments, savor the moment, and allow yourself to feel proud of what you've achieved.

Surrounding Yourself with Inspiration

Surrounding yourself with inspiration is another powerful way to build motivation and momentum. Whether it's through books, podcasts, quotes, or people, surrounding yourself with sources of inspiration can fuel your passion and keep you focused on your goals. Here are some ways to surround yourself with inspiration:

Read Inspirational Books and Articles

Seek out books, articles, and blogs that inspire and motivate you. Look for stories of people who have overcome obstacles, achieved their dreams, and made a positive impact in the world. Draw inspiration from their experiences and apply their lessons to your own journey.

Listen to Motivational Podcasts and Talks

Listen to podcasts and talks that uplift and inspire you. Look for speakers and topics that resonate with your goals and aspirations, and listen to them regularly for a dose of motivation and encouragement.

Surround Yourself with Positive People

Surround yourself with people who support and encourage your goals and aspirations. Seek out mentors, peers, and friends who share your values and inspire you to be your best self. Surrounding yourself with positive influences can help keep you motivated and focused on your goals.

Create an Inspiring Environment

Create an environment that fosters creativity, inspiration, and productivity. Surround yourself with things that inspire you, such as artwork, quotes, or photos of loved ones. Make your workspace a place where you feel motivated and energized to tackle your goals.

Conclusion

Building motivation and momentum is essential for overcoming procrastination and staying on track towards your goals. By understanding what motivates you, setting meaningful goals, and creating systems of accountability and support, you can cultivate a mindset of resilience and determination that empowers you to achieve success in all areas of your life.

In the next chapter, we'll explore practical strategies for overcoming distractions and staying focused on your goals, even when faced with challenges and obstacles. Through intentional action and a commitment to building motivation and momentum, you can unlock your full potential and create the life you desire.

CHAPTER TEN
OVERCOMING DISTRACTIONS
Focus: Avoiding Obstacles to Your Objectives

Distractions are a common obstacle on the path to productivity and success. Whether it's the ping of a new email, the lure of social media, or the chatter of coworkers, distractions can derail our focus and undermine our efforts to achieve our goals. In this chapter, we'll explore practical strategies for overcoming distractions and staying focused on our objectives, even in the face of constant interruptions and temptations.

Identifying Common Distractions

Before we can effectively overcome distractions, it's important to identify the most common sources of distraction in our lives. Distractions can come in many forms, including:

Digital Distractions

Digital distractions, such as email, social media, and smartphone notifications, are ubiquitous in today's hyper-connected world. The constant barrage of digital stimuli can make it difficult to maintain focus and concentration on our tasks.

Environmental Distractions

Environmental distractions, such as noise, clutter, and interruptions from coworkers or family members, can disrupt our concentration and make it challenging to stay focused on our work.

Internal Distractions

Internal distractions, such as negative thoughts, worries, and daydreams, can also undermine our focus and productivity. When our minds wander or become preoccupied with concerns unrelated to our tasks, it can be difficult to stay on track and maintain momentum.

Implementing Distraction-Blocking Techniques

Once we've identified the sources of distraction in our lives, we can begin implementing strategies to block or minimize their impact on our productivity. Here are some effective distraction-blocking techniques to consider:

Digital Detox

Consider implementing a digital detox by temporarily disconnecting from technology and minimizing your exposure to digital distractions. Turn off email notifications, silence your smartphone, and log out of social media to create a distraction-free work environment.

Set Boundaries

Set clear boundaries around your work time and space to minimize interruptions and distractions. Communicate your boundaries to coworkers, family members, and friends, and ask for their support in respecting your need for focus and concentration.

Create a Distraction-Free Workspace

Designate a specific workspace that is free from distractions and conducive to productivity. Keep your workspace tidy and organized, minimize noise and interruptions, and eliminate potential sources of distraction to create an environment that fosters concentration and focus.

Time-Blocking

Time-blocking is a time management technique that involves scheduling specific blocks of time for different tasks and activities. By allocating time to specific tasks and protecting that time from distractions and interruptions, you can increase your focus and productivity. Here's how to use time-blocking effectively:

- **Identify Your Most Productive Hours:** Identify your most productive hours, when you're alert, focused, and energized. Schedule your most important tasks during these times to maximize your productivity and make the most of your peak performance periods.

- **Allocate Time for Important Tasks:** Block out time in your schedule for important tasks and activities, such as work projects, exercise, and self-care. Prioritize these blocks of time and protect them from distractions and interruptions to ensure that you can focus fully on the task at hand.
- **Schedule Breaks and Downtime:** In addition to scheduling time for work and productivity, don't forget to schedule breaks and downtime to rest and recharge. Taking regular breaks helps prevent burnout and improves overall productivity and well-being. Include short breaks throughout your day and schedule longer breaks for meals, exercise, and relaxation.

Distraction-Free Tools and Apps

Use distraction-free tools and apps to minimize digital distractions and stay focused on your tasks. There are many apps available that can help block distracting websites, limit screen time, and track your productivity. Experiment with different tools and apps to find the ones that work best for you and incorporate them into your workflow.

Creating an Optimal Work Environment

Creating an optimal work environment is essential for minimizing distractions and maximizing productivity. Here are some tips for creating a distraction-free work environment:

Choose a Quiet Location

Choose a quiet location for your workspace, free from noise and interruptions. If possible, close the door or use noise-canceling headphones to block out distractions and create a peaceful environment conducive to focus and concentration.

Minimize Clutter

Keep your workspace tidy and organized to minimize visual clutter and distractions. Clear away unnecessary items from your desk, file papers and documents neatly, and create a clean, clutter-free environment that promotes productivity and focus.

Set Up Ergonomic Workspace

Set up an ergonomic workspace that supports good posture and comfort. Choose a comfortable chair with proper lumbar support, position your computer monitor at eye level to reduce neck strain, and use ergonomic accessories such as a keyboard tray and mouse pad to prevent repetitive strain injuries.

Conclusion

Distractions are a common challenge in today's fast-paced world, but with the right strategies and techniques, we can minimize their impact on our productivity and focus. By identifying the sources of distraction in our lives, implementing distraction-blocking techniques, and creating an optimal work environment, we can stay focused on our goals and achieve success in all areas of our lives.

In the next chapter, we'll explore practical strategies for managing procrastination and staying on track towards our objectives, even in the face of challenges and obstacles. Through intentional action and a commitment to overcoming distractions, we can unlock our full potential and create the life we desire.

CHAPTER ELEVEN
HANDLING PROCRASTINATION IN DIFFERENT AREAS OF LIFE
Focus: Compartmentalize and Categorize

Procrastination is a pervasive challenge that can affect various aspects of our lives, from academics and work to personal projects and health. In this chapter, we'll delve deeper into practical strategies for managing procrastination in different areas of life, providing comprehensive guidance to help individuals overcome obstacles and achieve their goals effectively.

Academics and Work

In academic and work settings, procrastination can have significant consequences, ranging from missed deadlines to compromised performance. Therefore, it's crucial to employ effective strategies to mitigate procrastination and maintain productivity. Let's explore some practical approaches:

Setting Clear Goals and Deadlines

Setting clear goals and deadlines is paramount for managing procrastination in academics and work. Break down larger projects into smaller, manageable tasks, and establish deadlines for each stage of the process. This not only provides a roadmap for progress but also instills a sense of accountability, motivating individuals to stay on track.

Creating a Productive Workspace

Creating a conducive workspace is essential for minimizing distractions and fostering productivity. Choose a quiet, organized environment that is free from interruptions, and ensure that you have all necessary resources readily available. By optimizing your workspace, you can create an atmosphere that promotes focus and concentration.

Utilizing Time Management Techniques

Effective time management is a cornerstone of combating procrastination. Techniques such as time-blocking and the Pomodoro Technique can help individuals allocate time efficiently and maintain momentum. By dedicating specific intervals to focused work and incorporating regular breaks, individuals can enhance productivity and reduce the likelihood of procrastination.

Seeking Support and Accountability

Seeking support and accountability from peers, mentors, or colleagues can provide valuable encouragement and motivation. Share your goals and deadlines with others, and establish regular check-ins to track progress and address challenges. By fostering a supportive network, individuals can stay motivated and accountable in their academic and professional pursuits.

Personal Projects and Hobbies

While personal projects and hobbies are often pursued for enjoyment and fulfillment, procrastination can still pose a barrier to progress. Here are some strategies for overcoming procrastination in these areas:

Finding Intrinsic Motivation

Intrinsic motivation, stemming from personal values and interests, is a powerful force for combating procrastination. Identify the aspects of your projects or hobbies that resonate most deeply with you, and focus on those elements to maintain enthusiasm and engagement. By connecting with your intrinsic motivation, you can sustain momentum and overcome procrastination more effectively.

Breaking Tasks into Smaller Steps

Breaking down projects and hobbies into smaller, manageable tasks can make them feel less daunting and more achievable. Set clear, attainable goals for each step of the process, and celebrate progress along the way. By tackling tasks incrementally, individuals can maintain momentum and prevent procrastination from derailing their efforts.

Creating a Supportive Environment

Surrounding yourself with resources and inspiration that support your projects and hobbies can bolster motivation and minimize procrastination. Cultivate a workspace or creative area that is conducive to your endeavors, and seek out communities or groups that share your interests. By immersing yourself in a supportive environment, you can stay motivated and focused on your goals.

Practicing Self-Compassion

Practicing self-compassion is essential for navigating the ups and downs of personal projects and hobbies. Be gentle with yourself when setbacks occur, and acknowledge that progress is not always linear. Celebrate successes, no matter how small, and embrace the learning process as an integral part of your journey. By cultivating self-compassion, individuals can overcome procrastination with resilience and kindness.

Health and Wellness

Procrastination in the realm of health and wellness can undermine individuals' efforts to prioritize self-care and maintain well-being. Here are strategies for overcoming procrastination in this area:

Setting Realistic Goals

Setting realistic and achievable health and wellness goals is crucial for combating procrastination. Break larger objectives, such as exercising regularly or adopting a nutritious diet, into smaller, actionable steps that can be integrated into daily routines. By setting attainable targets and celebrating progress, individuals can stay motivated and focused on their health goals.

Establishing Habits and Routines

Establishing healthy habits and routines is key to minimizing procrastination and promoting consistency in health-related behaviors. Create a structured schedule for exercise, meal planning, and self-care activities, and prioritize these practices as non-negotiable components of your daily routine. By embedding healthy habits into your lifestyle, you can reduce the temptation to procrastinate and make sustained progress towards your wellness goals.

Seeking Support and Accountability

Seeking support and accountability from peers, family members, or healthcare professionals can provide valuable encouragement and reinforcement in health and wellness endeavors. Share your goals and challenges with others, and enlist their support in holding you accountable for maintaining healthy habits. Regular check-ins help individuals stay motivated and committed to their objectives.

Practicing Mindfulness and Self-Care

Mindfulness and self-care practices are essential for managing stress and promoting overall well-being. Take time each day to engage in activities that nourish your mind, body, and spirit, such as meditation, yoga, or spending time in nature. By prioritizing self-care and cultivating mindfulness, individuals can reduce anxiety, enhance resilience, and overcome procrastination with ease.

Conclusion

Procrastination can manifest in various areas of life, posing challenges to individuals' academic, professional, personal, and health-related pursuits. By implementing tailored strategies for managing procrastination in each domain, individuals can enhance productivity, maintain motivation, and achieve goals effectively.

Whether it's setting clear goals and deadlines, finding intrinsic motivation, or seeking support and accountability, there are numerous approaches to overcoming procrastination and unlocking one's full potential in every aspect of life.

In the next chapter, we'll delve into strategies for coping with procrastination-induced stress and maintaining resilience in the face of challenges and setbacks. Through intentional action and a commitment to personal growth, individuals can overcome procrastination and cultivate a life filled with purpose, passion, and fulfillment.

CHAPTER TWELVE
MANAGING PROCRASTINATION IN RELATIONSHIPS
Focus: Communication and Collaboration

Procrastination isn't just limited to academic or work-related tasks; it can also seep into our personal relationships, affecting communication, collaboration, and overall harmony. In this chapter, we'll delve deeper into the dynamics of procrastination within relationships and provide practical strategies for managing it effectively.

Understanding the Impact of Procrastination

Procrastination can have a profound impact on relationships, eroding trust, causing frustration, and hindering effective communication. When tasks are consistently delayed or neglected, it can lead to feelings of resentment and discord, undermining the foundation of the relationship. Additionally, procrastination can create a sense of imbalance in the division of labor, with one partner feeling burdened by the responsibilities left unattended.

Recognizing Patterns

It's essential to recognize the signs of procrastination within the relationship, such as missed deadlines, unfinished projects, or repeated delays in fulfilling commitments. By acknowledging these patterns, individuals can take proactive steps to address them and prevent further strain on the relationship.

Understanding Root Causes

Procrastination within relationships can stem from various underlying factors, including fear of failure, perfectionism, or a lack of prioritization. By understanding the root causes of procrastination, individuals can begin to address the underlying issues and develop strategies for managing them effectively.

Communicating Needs and Boundaries

Communication is the cornerstone of healthy relationships, and addressing procrastination requires open and honest dialogue. Here are some ways to effectively communicate needs and boundaries:

Expressing Concerns

If you notice procrastination patterns affecting your relationship, express your concerns to your partner or loved one in a non-judgmental manner. Use "I" statements to convey your feelings and observations without placing blame or criticism.

Setting Clear Expectations

Clarify expectations regarding shared responsibilities, deadlines, and commitments within the relationship. Establishing clear guidelines helps reduce ambiguity and minimizes the potential for misunderstandings that can lead to procrastination.

Negotiating Solutions

Work together to identify solutions for addressing procrastination and fostering accountability within the relationship. Brainstorm strategies for managing tasks collaboratively, such as creating shared to-do lists or setting regular check-ins to monitor progress.

Collaborating Effectively with Others

Procrastination can also impact collaborative efforts within relationships, whether it's with a romantic partner, family member, or friend. Here are some strategies for fostering effective collaboration:

Delegating Tasks

Divide tasks and responsibilities based on individual strengths and preferences, and delegate accordingly. By distributing the workload evenly, you can prevent overwhelm and reduce the likelihood of procrastination.

Establishing a Team Mentality

Approach tasks and challenges as a team, emphasizing mutual support, cooperation, and accountability. Cultivate a sense of unity and shared purpose within the relationship, fostering a supportive environment where everyone feels valued and empowered to contribute.

Celebrating Achievements

Celebrate achievements and milestones together, acknowledging the collective effort and contributions of each person involved. By recognizing and celebrating progress, you reinforce positive behaviors and motivate continued collaboration.

Balancing Personal and Relationship Goals

Finding a balance between personal aspirations and relationship commitments is essential for managing procrastination in relationships. Here's how to strike that balance effectively:

Prioritizing Quality Time

Make time for meaningful connections and quality interactions with your partner or loved ones. Schedule regular date nights, family outings, or bonding activities to nurture the relationship and strengthen your emotional connection.

Honoring Individual Goals

Respect each other's individual goals, aspirations, and boundaries within the relationship. Encourage personal growth and self-expression, supporting each other's pursuits while also maintaining a sense of togetherness and mutual support.

Collaborative Goal-Setting

Set shared goals and aspirations as a couple or family unit, aligning your vision for the future and working towards common objectives together. Establishing shared goals fosters a sense of unity and purpose, motivating collective action and minimizing procrastination.

Conclusion

Managing procrastination in relationships requires effective communication, collaboration, and a commitment to mutual support and accountability. By openly addressing concerns, setting clear expectations, and fostering effective collaboration, individuals can overcome procrastination and strengthen connections with others. Finding a balance between personal and relationship goals is essential, prioritizing quality time together while honoring individual aspirations and boundaries.

Through intentional effort and a shared commitment to growth and mutual support, individuals can cultivate healthy, fulfilling relationships free from the constraints of procrastination.

In the next chapter, we'll explore strategies for coping with procrastination-induced stress and maintaining resilience in the face of challenges within relationships. Through compassionate communication and collaborative problem-solving, individuals can navigate the complexities of procrastination and nurture thriving relationships built on trust, understanding, and mutual support.

CHAPTER THIRTEEN
COPING WITH PROCRASTINATION-INDUCED STRESS
*Focus: The Toll It Takes,
and Ways to Deal With It*

Procrastination often leads to stress, creating a cycle of avoidance and anxiety that can be difficult to break. In this chapter, we'll delve into the psychological and emotional toll of procrastination and provide practical strategies for coping with procrastination-induced stress.

Understanding Procrastination-Induced Stress

Procrastination-induced stress is the result of delaying tasks or responsibilities, leading to increased pressure and anxiety as deadlines approach. This stress can manifest in various ways, including:

Anxiety and Worry

Procrastination can trigger feelings of anxiety and worry, as individuals anticipate the consequences of their delayed actions. The fear of failure or disappointment can weigh heavily on the mind, making it difficult to focus and concentrate on tasks.

Guilt and Shame

Feelings of guilt and shame are common among procrastinators, who may berate themselves for their perceived laziness or lack of discipline. These negative emotions can further exacerbate stress and undermine self-esteem, creating a vicious cycle of avoidance and self-criticism.

Physical Symptoms

Procrastination-induced stress can also manifest in physical symptoms such as tension headaches, muscle stiffness, and digestive issues. The body's physiological response to stress can take a toll on overall health and well-being, further complicating the procrastination cycle.

Stress Management Techniques

Coping with procrastination-induced stress requires proactive strategies for managing anxiety, promoting relaxation, and fostering resilience. Here are some effective stress management techniques to consider:

Mindfulness and Meditation Practices

Mindfulness and meditation practices can help individuals cultivate present-moment awareness and reduce stress levels. By focusing on the breath and observing thoughts without judgment, individuals can develop a greater sense of calm and equanimity in the face of procrastination-induced stress.

Stress-Relief Activities

Engaging in stress-relief activities such as exercise, yoga, or creative expression can help alleviate tension and promote relaxation. Physical activity releases endorphins, the body's natural stress relievers, while creative outlets provide a means of self-expression and emotional release.

Deep Breathing Exercises

Deep breathing exercises can help activate the body's relaxation response, counteracting the physiological effects of stress. Practice diaphragmatic breathing techniques, such as belly breathing or 4-7-8 breathing, to promote feelings of calm and reduce anxiety.

Progressive Muscle Relaxation

Progressive muscle relaxation involves tensing and releasing muscle groups throughout the body to promote physical and mental relaxation. Start by tensing the muscles in your feet and gradually work your way up to your head, releasing tension with each exhalation.

Visualization Techniques

Visualization techniques involve mentally picturing a peaceful scene or scenario to evoke feelings of relaxation and tranquility. Close your eyes and imagine yourself in a serene environment, such as a beach or forest, and focus on the sights, sounds, and sensations of that place.

Seeking Support and Professional Help

If procrastination-induced stress becomes overwhelming or significantly impacts daily functioning, seeking support from loved ones or mental health professionals can be beneficial. Here are some options to consider:

Talking to a Trusted Friend or Family Member

Reach out to a trusted friend or family member and share your concerns about procrastination-induced stress. Sometimes, simply talking about your feelings with someone who cares can provide a sense of relief and perspective.

Seeking Therapy or Counseling

Therapy or counseling can provide individuals with tools and techniques for managing procrastination-induced stress and addressing underlying issues contributing to procrastination. Cognitive-behavioral therapy (CBT) and mindfulness-based approaches have been shown to be particularly effective in treating stress-related procrastination.

Exploring Stress-Reduction Techniques

Explore stress-reduction techniques such as relaxation training, biofeedback, or stress management workshops. These interventions can help individuals develop coping skills and resilience strategies for managing procrastination-induced stress more effectively.

Cultivating Self-Compassion

Cultivating self-compassion is essential for coping with procrastination-induced stress and fostering resilience in the face of setbacks. Here's how to practice self-compassion:

Acknowledging Imperfection

Recognize that everyone experiences procrastination and stress at times, and that it's okay to be imperfect. Embrace your humanity and acknowledge that setbacks and challenges are a natural part of the human experience.

Treating Yourself with Kindness

Be kind and compassionate towards yourself, especially when facing procrastination-induced stress. Practice self-care activities that nourish your mind, body, and spirit, and prioritize activities that bring you joy and fulfillment.

Reframing Negative Self-Talk

Challenge negative self-talk and replace it with more compassionate and supportive language. Instead of berating yourself for procrastination, remind yourself that you're doing the best you can in the moment, and that setbacks are opportunities for growth and learning.

Conclusion

Procrastination-induced stress can take a significant toll on individuals' mental, emotional, and physical well-being. By understanding the psychological and emotional impact of procrastination, and implementing effective stress management techniques, individuals can cope more effectively with the challenges of procrastination-induced stress.

Whether it's practicing mindfulness and meditation, seeking support from loved ones or mental health professionals, or cultivating self-compassion, there are numerous strategies for managing procrastination-induced stress and promoting overall resilience and well-being.

In the next chapter, we'll explore strategies for building consistency and discipline to overcome procrastination and achieve long-term success in various areas of life.

CHAPTER FOURTEEN
DEVELOPING CONSISTENCY AND DISCIPLINE
Focus: Routines For Success

Consistency and discipline are the cornerstones of overcoming procrastination and achieving long-term success in various areas of life. In this chapter, we'll explore the importance of consistency and discipline, and provide practical strategies for developing these qualities to combat procrastination effectively.

Understanding Consistency and Discipline

Consistency refers to the ability to maintain regularity and steadfastness in one's actions, habits, and routines over time. Discipline, on the other hand, involves the capacity to exert self-control, focus, and perseverance in pursuit of goals and objectives, even in the face of challenges or distractions.

The Importance of Consistency

Consistency is crucial for building momentum and making progress towards goals. By consistently taking small, incremental steps towards objectives, individuals can create positive habits and routines that reinforce productivity and minimize the likelihood of procrastination.

The Value of Discipline

Discipline is essential for overcoming procrastination and staying focused on tasks and responsibilities. It involves setting priorities, establishing boundaries, and adhering to a structured plan of action, even when faced with temptations or obstacles that may lead to procrastination.

Strategies for Developing Consistency

Developing consistency requires intentional effort and commitment to establishing productive habits and routines. Here are some strategies to help cultivate consistency in various areas of life:

Establishing Clear Goals

Set clear, specific goals that align with your values and aspirations. Break down larger objectives into smaller, manageable tasks, and create a plan of action for achieving them. By setting clear goals, individuals can maintain focus and direction, minimizing the risk of procrastination.

Creating a Routine

Establishing a daily routine helps provide structure and organization to your day, reducing the likelihood of procrastination. Identify key tasks and activities that contribute to your goals, and allocate dedicated time slots for each. Stick to your routine consistently to build momentum and reinforce positive habits.

Prioritizing Tasks

Prioritize tasks based on their importance and urgency, focusing on high-priority items first. Use techniques such as Eisenhower's Urgent/Important Principle or the ABCDE method to categorize tasks and allocate time and resources accordingly. By prioritizing effectively, individuals can ensure that essential tasks are completed promptly, reducing the risk of procrastination.

Setting Realistic Expectations

Set realistic expectations for yourself and your abilities, taking into account factors such as time constraints, resources, and competing priorities. Avoid overcommitting or setting unattainable goals, as this can lead to feelings of overwhelm and increase the likelihood of procrastination. Instead, set achievable targets that stretch your abilities without causing undue stress.

Strategies for Developing Discipline

Developing discipline requires practice and perseverance, as well as a willingness to challenge limiting beliefs and habits. Here are some strategies to help cultivate discipline and overcome procrastination:

Building Self-Awareness

Develop self-awareness by reflecting on your thoughts, emotions, and behaviors related to procrastination. Identify patterns, triggers, and underlying reasons for procrastination, and explore strategies for addressing them effectively. By understanding your procrastination tendencies, you can develop targeted interventions to cultivate discipline and self-control.

Practicing Delayed Gratification

Practice delayed gratification by delaying immediate rewards in favor of long-term goals and objectives. Learn to tolerate discomfort and uncertainty, and resist the urge to give in to short-term impulses or distractions. By focusing on the bigger picture and prioritizing long-term benefits over immediate pleasures, individuals can cultivate discipline and resilience in the face of temptation.

Implementing Accountability Measures

Create systems of accountability to help reinforce discipline and commitment to your goals. Share your goals and progress with trusted friends, family members, or mentors, and enlist their support in holding you accountable for staying on track. Regular check-ins and progress updates can help maintain motivation and focus, reducing the risk of procrastination.

Cultivating Self-Discipline Habits

Develop self-discipline habits by incorporating rituals and routines that promote focus, productivity, and self-control. Practice techniques such as time-blocking, setting deadlines, and eliminating distractions to create an environment conducive to disciplined action. By consistently practicing self-discipline habits, individuals can strengthen their willpower and overcome procrastination more effectively.

Overcoming Common Challenges

Developing consistency and discipline is not without its challenges, and individuals may encounter obstacles along the way. Here are some common challenges to be aware of, along with strategies for overcoming them:

Managing Procrastination

Procrastination is a common barrier to developing consistency and discipline. Identify the root causes of procrastination and implement targeted strategies for addressing them, such as setting deadlines, breaking tasks into smaller steps, and practicing self-awareness and self-compassion.

Dealing with Distractions

Distractions can derail efforts to maintain focus and discipline. Minimize distractions by creating a conducive work environment, utilizing productivity tools and techniques, and practicing mindfulness and concentration exercises. Set boundaries around your time and energy to protect your focus and avoid succumbing to distractions.

Maintaining Motivation

Maintaining motivation over the long term can be challenging, especially when faced with setbacks or obstacles. Cultivate intrinsic motivation by connecting with your values, passions, and purpose, and reminding yourself of the reasons behind your goals. Celebrate progress and milestones along the way to stay inspired and motivated to continue your journey.

Conclusion

Developing consistency and discipline is essential for overcoming procrastination and achieving long-term success in various areas of life. By setting clear goals, establishing routines, prioritizing tasks, and cultivating self-discipline habits, individuals can build momentum and make progress towards their objectives.

Although challenges may arise along the way, with perseverance, self-awareness, and a commitment to personal growth, individuals can overcome procrastination and cultivate a life characterized by consistency, discipline, and fulfillment.

In the next chapter, we'll explore strategies for overcoming perfectionism paralysis and embracing progress over perfection. Through intentional action and a willingness to embrace imperfection, individuals can overcome perfectionism and unlock their full potential in pursuit of their goals and aspirations.

CHAPTER FIFTEEN
OVERCOMING PERFECTIONISM PARALYSIS
Focus: Fight the Fear of Failure

Perfectionism is a double-edged sword; while it can drive individuals to strive for excellence, it can also lead to paralysis, as the fear of failure or imperfection prevents them from taking action. In this chapter, we'll delve into the phenomenon of perfectionism paralysis, explore its underlying causes, and provide practical strategies for overcoming it.

Understanding Perfectionism Paralysis

Perfectionism paralysis occurs when the pursuit of perfection inhibits individuals from taking action or making progress towards their goals. The fear of making mistakes, being judged, or falling short of unrealistic standards can immobilize individuals, trapping them in a cycle of indecision and inaction.

The Fear of Failure

At the heart of perfectionism paralysis lies the fear of failure. Perfectionists often equate mistakes or imperfections with personal inadequacy, leading them to avoid taking risks or making decisions that could result in failure. This fear of failure can paralyze individuals, preventing them from moving forward and realizing their full potential.

The All-or-Nothing Mindset

Perfectionists tend to adopt an all-or-nothing mindset, viewing success and failure in black-and-white terms. They believe that anything less than perfection is unacceptable, leading them to set impossibly high standards for themselves and others. This rigid thinking pattern contributes to perfectionism paralysis, as individuals become consumed by the quest for flawlessness.

Analysis Paralysis

Analysis paralysis occurs when individuals become so preoccupied with evaluating and reevaluating their options that they are unable to make decisions or take action. Perfectionists may overanalyze every detail, seeking certainty and reassurance before moving forward. This excessive rumination and second-guessing can stall progress and perpetuate feelings of uncertainty and indecision.

Recognizing the Signs of Perfectionism Paralysis

Perfectionism paralysis can manifest in various ways, both internally and externally. Here are some common signs to watch out for:

Procrastination

Procrastination is a hallmark sign of perfectionism paralysis. Perfectionists may delay taking action on tasks or projects indefinitely, waiting for the perfect moment or circumstances to begin. This procrastination is often fueled by the fear of making mistakes or falling short of unrealistic standards.

Over-Planning

Perfectionists may engage in excessive planning and preparation, seeking to anticipate and control every possible outcome. While planning can be helpful, perfectionists may become trapped in a cycle of over-planning, obsessing over minute details and potential pitfalls.

Self-Doubt and Self-Criticism

Perfectionists are often plagued by self-doubt and self-criticism, constantly questioning their abilities and worthiness. They may harshly judge themselves for perceived shortcomings or mistakes, undermining their confidence and self-esteem.

Avoidance of Challenges

Perfectionists may avoid taking on new challenges or opportunities for fear of failure or criticism. They may stick to familiar tasks or routines where they feel safe and in control, missing out on valuable opportunities for growth and development.

Strategies for Overcoming Perfectionism Paralysis

Overcoming perfectionism paralysis requires a combination of self-awareness, self-compassion, and targeted interventions. Here are some practical strategies to help individuals break free from the grip of perfectionism and take meaningful action towards their goals:

Challenge All-or-Nothing Thinking

Challenge the all-or-nothing mindset by recognizing that perfection is an unrealistic and unattainable standard. Embrace the concept of "good enough" and acknowledge that mistakes and imperfections are a natural part of the learning process. Reframe failures as opportunities for growth and learning, rather than reflections of personal inadequacy.

Practice Self-Compassion

Cultivate self-compassion by treating yourself with kindness and understanding, especially in moments of difficulty or setback. Practice self-acceptance and acknowledge your inherent worthiness, regardless of external achievements or validation. Be gentle with yourself and recognize that you are worthy of love and compassion, regardless of your perceived flaws or mistakes.

Break Tasks into Smaller Steps

Break tasks or projects into smaller, more manageable steps to avoid feeling overwhelmed or intimidated. Focus on taking one small action at a time, rather than trying to tackle the entire task at once. This approach helps build momentum and confidence, making it easier to overcome perfectionism paralysis and make progress towards your goals.

Set Realistic Goals

Set realistic, achievable goals that align with your values and priorities. Avoid setting overly ambitious or perfectionistic goals that are bound to lead to disappointment or frustration. Instead, set SMART goals (Specific, Measurable, Achievable, Relevant, Time-bound) that are challenging yet attainable, allowing for flexibility and adaptability as needed.

Embrace Imperfection

Embrace imperfection as a natural and inevitable part of the human experience. Recognize that perfection is an illusion and that striving for flawlessness is both futile and counterproductive. Embrace the beauty of imperfection and celebrate your progress, even if it falls short of your ideal standards.

Take Imperfect Action

Take imperfect action by embracing the mantra of "progress over perfection." Focus on taking consistent, purposeful action towards your goals, even if it means making mistakes or encountering setbacks along the way. Remember that imperfect action is better than no action at all, and that each step forward brings you closer to your desired outcome.

Cultivate a Growth Mindset

Cultivate a growth mindset by adopting a positive attitude towards learning and personal development. Embrace challenges as opportunities for growth and view failures as valuable learning experiences. Cultivate resilience and perseverance in the face of setbacks, knowing that setbacks are temporary and can be overcome with persistence and determination.

Practice Self-Reflection

Engage in regular self-reflection to identify and challenge perfectionistic tendencies. Reflect on your thoughts, feelings, and behaviors related to procrastination and perfectionism, and explore alternative perspectives and coping strategies. Cultivate self-awareness and mindfulness to better understand your triggers and patterns, allowing you to respond more effectively in challenging situations.

Seek Support and Accountability

Seek support from trusted friends, family members, or mentors who can offer encouragement, guidance, and accountability as you work to overcome perfectionism paralysis. Share your goals and challenges with others, and enlist their support in holding you accountable for taking action and making progress towards your goals.

Practice Gradual Exposure

Practice gradual exposure to situations or tasks that trigger perfectionism paralysis, starting with small, manageable steps and gradually increasing the level of challenge over time. By gradually exposing yourself to perceived threats or discomfort, you can desensitize yourself to perfectionistic fears and build confidence in your ability to cope with uncertainty and imperfection.

Celebrate Progress, Not Perfection

Celebrate your progress and accomplishments, no matter how small or incremental they may seem. Recognize and acknowledge your efforts and achievements, and take pride in the progress you've made towards your goals. Cultivate a sense of gratitude and appreciation for the journey, embracing the process of growth and self-discovery.

Conclusion

Perfectionism paralysis can be a significant barrier to achieving your goals and realizing your full potential. By understanding the underlying causes of perfectionism paralysis and implementing practical strategies for overcoming it, you can break free from the grip of perfectionism and take meaningful action towards your goals. By challenging all-or-nothing thinking, practicing self-compassion, breaking tasks into smaller steps, setting realistic goals, and embracing imperfection, you can cultivate a mindset of progress over perfection.

CHAPTER SIXTEEN
EMBRACING CREATIVITY AND INNOVATION
Focus: Imperfection is Acceptable, Now What?

Creativity and innovation are essential for breaking free from the constraints of perfectionism and unlocking your full potential. In this chapter, we'll explore the role of creativity and innovation in overcoming perfectionism, and provide practical strategies for fostering creativity and embracing innovation in pursuit of your goals.

Understanding the Role of Creativity and Innovation

Creativity is the ability to generate novel ideas, solutions, or expressions, while innovation involves implementing those ideas to create value. Both creativity and innovation are essential for overcoming perfectionism, as they encourage experimentation, flexibility, and adaptation to change.

Breaking Free from Perfectionism

Creativity and innovation provide an alternative to the rigid standards and expectations of perfectionism. By embracing creativity, individuals can explore new possibilities, challenge conventional thinking, and break free from the limitations of perfectionistic thinking patterns.

Embracing Imperfection

Creativity and innovation thrive in environments where imperfection is accepted and even celebrated. By embracing imperfection as a natural and necessary part of the creative process, individuals can overcome the fear of failure and perfectionism paralysis that often inhibit innovation.

Fostering Growth Mindset

Creativity and innovation are closely linked to a growth mindset, which emphasizes the belief that abilities and intelligence can be developed through effort and perseverance. By cultivating a growth mindset, individuals can adopt a more flexible and open attitude towards challenges and setbacks, enabling them to approach problems with curiosity and resilience.

Cultivating Creativity

Cultivating creativity involves nurturing an environment that fosters imagination, experimentation, and originality. Here are some strategies for fostering creativity in your personal and professional life:

Engage in Creative Activities

Participate in activities that inspire creativity, such as painting, writing, music, or cooking. Allow yourself to explore new mediums and techniques without worrying about perfection or judgment. The goal is to express yourself freely and tap into your innate creative potential.

Practice Divergent Thinking

Practice divergent thinking by generating multiple ideas or solutions to a problem without judgment or evaluation. Brainstorming, mind mapping, or freewriting are effective techniques for unlocking creative insights and exploring unconventional possibilities.

Seek Inspiration from Diverse Sources

Expose yourself to diverse sources of inspiration, including art, literature, nature, and culture. Explore different perspectives, styles, and disciplines to stimulate your imagination and expand your creative repertoire. Drawing connections between seemingly unrelated ideas can spark innovative solutions and breakthroughs.

Embrace Playfulness and Curiosity

Approach challenges with a sense of playfulness and curiosity, allowing yourself to experiment, take risks, and make mistakes along the way. Play is essential for fostering creativity, as it encourages exploration, spontaneity, and unconventional thinking.

Embracing Innovation

Embracing innovation involves applying creative ideas and solutions to create value and drive positive change. Here are some strategies for embracing innovation in your personal and professional endeavors:

Identify Opportunities for Improvement

Identify areas in your life or work where innovation could lead to meaningful improvements or advancements. Look for inefficiencies, pain points, or unmet needs that could be addressed through innovative solutions or approaches.

Encourage Collaboration and Diversity

Encourage collaboration and diversity of thought by seeking input and perspectives from a diverse range of individuals. Collaborative problem-solving and idea generation can lead to more innovative solutions by leveraging the collective knowledge, skills, and experiences of a group.

Experiment and Iterate

Embrace a culture of experimentation and iteration, where failure is viewed as a natural and necessary part of the innovation process. Test out new ideas, gather feedback, and iterate based on insights and learnings gained from each experiment. Rapid prototyping and agile methodologies can help accelerate the innovation cycle and drive continuous improvement.

Embrace Failure as a Learning Opportunity

Shift your perspective on failure from a negative outcome to a valuable learning opportunity. Embrace a growth mindset that views failure as an essential step on the path to success. Analyze failures objectively, extract lessons learned, and use them to inform future innovation efforts.

Overcoming Perfectionism in the Creative Process

Overcoming perfectionism in the creative process requires a shift in mindset and approach. Here are some strategies for navigating the challenges of perfectionism and embracing creativity and innovation:

Set Realistic Expectations

Set realistic expectations for your creative endeavors, recognizing that perfection is neither achievable nor desirable. Focus on progress over perfection, celebrating incremental improvements and learning from setbacks along the way.

Embrace Iteration and Revision

Embrace iteration and revision as integral parts of the creative process. Allow yourself to experiment, explore, and refine your ideas through multiple iterations. Recognize that the first draft or prototype is rarely perfect and that refinement is a natural and necessary part of the creative journey.

Practice Self-Compassion

Practice self-compassion by treating yourself with kindness and understanding, especially when faced with creative challenges or setbacks. Be gentle with yourself and acknowledge that creativity is a journey of exploration and discovery, not a destination to be reached.

Seek Feedback and Support

Seek feedback and support from trusted peers, mentors, or collaborators who can offer constructive criticism and encouragement. Embrace feedback as an opportunity for growth and learning, recognizing that external perspectives can help you see your work from new angles and identify areas for improvement.

Conclusion

Creativity and innovation are powerful antidotes to perfectionism, offering pathways to self-expression, growth, and fulfillment. By embracing creativity, individuals can break free from the constraints of perfectionism and unlock their full potential to innovate and create value in their personal and professional lives. Cultivating creativity involves nurturing an environment that fosters imagination, experimentation, and originality, while embracing innovation requires applying creative ideas and solutions to drive positive change. By practicing divergent thinking, seeking inspiration from diverse sources, and embracing experimentation and iteration, individuals can overcome perfectionism and embrace the joy of creative expression and innovation.

In the next chapter, we'll explore the role of procrastination in the creative process and provide strategies for harnessing procrastination tendencies to enhance creativity and productivity. Through intentional action and a willingness to embrace imperfection, individuals can cultivate a creative mindset that empowers them to explore new possibilities, solve complex problems, and make meaningful contributions to the world around them.

CHAPTER SEVENTEEN
THE ROLE OF PROCRASTINATION IN THE CREATIVE PROCESS
Focus: What Is Procrastination?

Procrastination is often viewed as a barrier to productivity and creativity, but it can also play a significant role in the creative process. In this chapter, we'll explore how procrastination can both hinder and facilitate creativity, and provide strategies for harnessing procrastination tendencies to enhance creative thinking and productivity.

Understanding Procrastination

Procrastination is the act of delaying or postponing tasks or activities, often due to feelings of anxiety, fear, or avoidance. It is commonly associated with negative outcomes, such as missed deadlines, increased stress, and decreased productivity. However, procrastination is a complex phenomenon that can have both positive and negative effects on the creative process.

Types of Procrastination

1. **Active Procrastination:** Some individuals thrive under pressure and intentionally delay tasks until the last minute, using the adrenaline rush of a looming deadline to fuel their productivity.

2. **Passive Procrastination:** Others may avoid tasks altogether, putting off important activities indefinitely due to fear of failure, perfectionism, or overwhelm.

The Dark Side of Procrastination

Procrastination can pose significant challenges to the creative process, including:

Increased Stress and Anxiety

Procrastination often leads to increased stress and anxiety as deadlines approach and tasks remain unfinished. The pressure to complete work under tight timelines can undermine creativity and lead to rushed, subpar outcomes.

Loss of Momentum

Procrastination disrupts the flow of creative energy and momentum, making it difficult to sustain focus and motivation over time. Constantly starting and stopping tasks can fragment attention and hinder the development of ideas.

Missed Opportunities

Procrastination can result in missed opportunities for creative exploration and innovation. Delaying action on ideas or projects may mean missing out on valuable insights, collaborations, or breakthroughs.

The Bright Side of Procrastination

While procrastination is often viewed negatively, it can also serve as a catalyst for creativity and innovation. Here's how procrastination can benefit the creative process:

Incubation Period

Procrastination provides a built-in incubation period during which ideas have time to percolate and develop subconsciously. Stepping away from a project allows the mind to wander and make unexpected connections, leading to fresh perspectives and insights.

Creative Restlessness

Procrastination can manifest as a form of creative restlessness, driving individuals to seek out new experiences, stimuli, or challenges. Embracing this restlessness can lead to serendipitous encounters, inspirations, or breakthroughs that fuel creativity.

Play and Exploration

Procrastination offers opportunities for play and exploration, allowing individuals to experiment with ideas, materials, or techniques without the pressure of immediate deadlines or expectations. Playful experimentation can lead to unexpected discoveries and creative solutions.

Strategies for Harnessing Procrastination

Rather than viewing procrastination as an enemy to be defeated, it can be leveraged as a valuable ally in the creative process. Here are some strategies for harnessing procrastination tendencies to enhance creativity and productivity:

Set Realistic Deadlines

Set realistic deadlines for projects or tasks, allowing for ample time to explore ideas, iterate, and refine without feeling rushed or overwhelmed. Breaking larger projects into smaller, manageable chunks can make them feel less daunting and more achievable.

Embrace Structured Procrastination

Practice structured procrastination by prioritizing tasks based on their importance and urgency. Instead of avoiding important tasks altogether, procrastinate productively by working on less critical tasks while allowing ideas to simmer in the background.

Schedule Breaks and Downtime

Schedule regular breaks and downtime to recharge and rejuvenate the creative spirit. Taking time away from work allows the mind to rest and recharge, making it more receptive to new ideas and insights when returning to tasks.

Cultivate a Creative Environment

Create a conducive environment for creativity by surrounding yourself with inspiring stimuli, such as art, music, nature, or stimulating conversations. Designate a dedicated workspace that fosters focus and minimizes distractions, allowing for deep engagement with creative projects.

Overcoming Procrastination Paralysis

Procrastination paralysis occurs when the fear of failure or perfectionism prevents individuals from taking action on creative projects. Here are some strategies for overcoming procrastination paralysis:

Set Small, Achievable Goals

Break creative projects into smaller, more manageable tasks or milestones, making them feel less overwhelming and more attainable. Focus on making progress, however small, rather than aiming for perfection.

Create a Routine or Ritual

Establish a daily routine or ritual to signal to your brain that it's time to engage in creative work. Consistency and repetition can help overcome resistance and create a sense of momentum and continuity in your creative practice.

Practice Mindfulness and Self-Compassion

Cultivate mindfulness and self-compassion to counteract negative thought patterns and self-criticism associated with procrastination paralysis. Be gentle with yourself and recognize that creativity is a process that involves trial and error.

Conclusion

Procrastination can be both a hindrance and a catalyst for creativity, depending on how it's approached and managed. By understanding the different manifestations of procrastination and implementing strategies for harnessing its potential, individuals can leverage procrastination tendencies to enhance creativity and productivity in their creative pursuits. Whether it's allowing ideas to incubate subconsciously, embracing creative restlessness, or engaging in playful experimentation, procrastination can serve as a valuable ally in the creative process. By reframing procrastination as a natural and productive part of the creative journey, individuals can overcome perfectionism paralysis and unlock their full potential.

In the next chapter, we'll explore strategies for cultivating self-confidence and resilience in the face of creative challenges and setbacks. Through intentional action and a willingness to embrace the creative process, individuals can cultivate a mindset of curiosity, exploration, and innovation that empowers them to realize their creative vision and make meaningful contributions to the world around them.

CHAPTER EIGHTEEN
CULTIVATING SELF-CONFIDENCE
Focus: Building and Rebuilding Yourself

Self-confidence and resilience are essential qualities for navigating the ups and downs of the creative journey. In this chapter, we'll explore the importance of cultivating self-confidence and resilience in creative endeavors, and provide practical strategies for building these qualities to overcome challenges and setbacks.

Understanding Self-Confidence

Self-confidence is the belief in one's ability to successfully meet challenges, achieve goals, and handle adversity. It involves trusting in your skills, talents, and judgment, and having a positive self-image. In the context of creativity, self-confidence is crucial for taking risks, exploring new ideas, and expressing oneself authentically.

The Importance of Self-Confidence in Creativity

Self-confidence is essential for unleashing creativity and innovation. It empowers individuals to trust their instincts, take creative risks, and persevere in the face of uncertainty or criticism. With self-confidence, creators are more likely to overcome self-doubt and fear of failure, allowing them to fully engage in the creative process and express their unique voice.

Cultivating Self-Confidence

Cultivating self-confidence is a lifelong journey that requires self-awareness, practice, and resilience. Here are some strategies for building self-confidence in creative pursuits:

Recognize Your Strengths and Accomplishments

Take time to reflect on your strengths, talents, and past achievements. Celebrate your successes, no matter how small, and acknowledge your progress along the way. Keeping a journal or gratitude list can help reinforce positive self-talk and bolster self-confidence.

Set Realistic Goals

Set realistic, achievable goals that stretch your abilities without overwhelming you. Break larger goals into smaller, manageable steps, and celebrate each milestone as you progress. By setting and achieving goals, you'll build a sense of competence and confidence in your abilities.

Challenge Negative Self-Talk

Challenge negative self-talk and limiting beliefs that undermine your confidence. Replace self-critical thoughts with affirmations and positive self-statements that reinforce your worth and potential. Practice self-compassion and treat yourself with kindness and understanding, especially during times of self-doubt or adversity.

Seek Feedback and Support

Seek feedback and support from trusted mentors, peers, or collaborators who can offer constructive criticism and encouragement. Surround yourself with a supportive community of fellow creators who believe in your talents and cheer you on in your creative pursuits. Constructive feedback can help you grow and improve while boosting your confidence in your abilities.

Understanding Resilience

Resilience is the ability to bounce back from setbacks, adapt to change, and persevere in the face of adversity. It involves coping effectively with stress, maintaining a positive outlook, and bouncing back stronger from challenges. Resilience is crucial for navigating the inevitable ups and downs of the creative process and overcoming obstacles along the way.

The Importance of Resilience in Creativity

Creativity often involves facing rejection, criticism, and failure. Resilience enables creators to bounce back from setbacks, learn from mistakes, and keep moving forward in pursuit of their creative vision. With resilience, creators are better equipped to weather the inevitable challenges of the creative journey and emerge stronger and more resilient.

Building Resilience

Building resilience requires cultivating coping skills, fostering a growth mindset, and cultivating a supportive network. Here are some strategies for building resilience in creative endeavors:

Cultivate a Growth Mindset

Adopt a growth mindset that views challenges and setbacks as opportunities for growth and learning. Embrace failures as valuable learning experiences and reframing setbacks as temporary obstacles on the path to success. By cultivating a growth mindset, you'll develop the resilience to persevere in the face of adversity and bounce back stronger than before.

Develop Coping Skills

Develop coping skills to manage stress, anxiety, and self-doubt effectively. Practice relaxation techniques such as deep breathing, mindfulness meditation, or progressive muscle relaxation to calm your mind and body during times of stress. Engage in activities that bring you joy and relaxation, such as exercise, hobbies, or spending time in nature.

Build a Supportive Network

Build a supportive network of friends, family, mentors, and fellow creators who can offer encouragement, guidance, and emotional support. Surround yourself with people who believe in your talents and cheer you on in your creative pursuits. Lean on your support network during challenging times and share your successes and struggles openly with them.

Cultivate Adaptability

Cultivate adaptability by embracing change and uncertainty as inevitable parts of the creative journey. Stay flexible and open-minded in your approach to creative projects, allowing room for experimentation and iteration. Embrace new challenges as opportunities for growth and innovation, and be willing to pivot or adjust your plans as needed.

Overcoming Setbacks and Building Resilience

Setbacks are inevitable in the creative process, but they can also be valuable learning opportunities. Here are some strategies for overcoming setbacks and building resilience:

Learn from Mistakes

View mistakes and failures as opportunities for growth and learning. Analyze setbacks objectively, identify lessons learned, and use them to inform future creative endeavors. Embrace a growth mindset that recognizes that setbacks are temporary and can be overcome with perseverance and determination.

Reframe Setbacks

Reframe setbacks as temporary obstacles on the path to success. Instead of dwelling on failures or setbacks, focus on what you can learn from them and how you can use them to fuel your creative journey. Embrace setbacks as opportunities for growth, innovation, and self-discovery.

Build a Support System

Lean on your support system during challenging times and share your successes and struggles openly with them. Seek guidance, encouragement, and emotional support from trusted friends, family, mentors, or fellow creators who understand the creative process and believe in your talents.

Conclusion

Cultivating self-confidence and resilience is essential for navigating the challenges and uncertainties of the creative journey. By recognizing your strengths and accomplishments, setting realistic goals, challenging negative self-talk, and seeking feedback and support, you can build self-confidence in your creative abilities. Similarly, by fostering a growth mindset, developing coping skills, building a supportive network, and cultivating adaptability, you can build resilience to overcome setbacks and bounce back stronger than before.

In the next chapter, we'll explore the power of saying no and setting boundaries to protect your time, energy, and creative focus. Through intentional action and a commitment to self-care and personal growth, you can cultivate the confidence and resilience needed to thrive as a creator and make meaningful contributions to the world around you.

CHAPTER NINETEEN
NAVIGATING PERFECTIONISM IN A COMPETITIVE WORLD
Focus: Set Boundaries

In a world that often glorifies achievement and success, navigating perfectionism can be a significant challenge. In this chapter, we'll explore the impact of perfectionism in competitive environments and provide strategies for overcoming perfectionism tendencies to foster collaboration, innovation, and personal growth.

Understanding Perfectionism in a Competitive Context

Perfectionism is a double-edged sword in competitive environments, as it can drive individuals to excel but also lead to excessive self-criticism, fear of failure, and burnout. In competitive fields such as academia, business, or the arts, the pressure to succeed can exacerbate perfectionistic tendencies and create a culture of comparison and competition.

The Perfectionism-Competitiveness Connection

Perfectionism and competitiveness are often intertwined, as individuals may equate perfection with success and view competition as a measure of their worth. The desire to outperform others and achieve flawless results can fuel perfectionistic striving and intensify feelings of inadequacy or self-doubt when expectations are not met.

Comparing Yourself to Others

In competitive environments, individuals may fall into the trap of comparing themselves to others and measuring their success against external benchmarks. This constant comparison can breed feelings of insecurity, envy, or imposter syndrome, undermining self-confidence and eroding motivation.

Consequences of Perfectionism in a Competitive World

Perfectionism can have profound consequences in competitive environments, including:

Imposter Syndrome

Perfectionists may experience imposter syndrome, feeling like frauds or undeserving of their achievements despite evidence of competence or success. The fear of being exposed as inadequate can undermine self-confidence and lead to self-sabotage or burnout.

Fear of Failure

Perfectionists often harbor a deep-seated fear of failure, viewing mistakes or setbacks as evidence of personal inadequacy. The pressure to avoid failure at all costs can lead to risk aversion, procrastination, or avoidance behaviors that hinder growth and innovation.

Comparison and Competition

Perfectionists may become caught in a cycle of comparison and competition, constantly measuring themselves against others and striving for unattainable standards of excellence. This relentless pursuit of perfection can fuel stress, anxiety, and feelings of isolation or resentment towards peers.

Strategies for Navigating Perfectionism in a Competitive World

Navigating perfectionism in competitive environments requires a combination of self-awareness, self-compassion, and boundary-setting. Here are some strategies for overcoming perfectionism tendencies and fostering a healthier approach to competition:

Practice Self-Compassion

Practice self-compassion by treating yourself with kindness and understanding, especially during times of failure or setbacks. Cultivate a mindset of self-acceptance and recognize that your worth is not determined by external achievements or comparisons to others.

Set Realistic Expectations

Set realistic, achievable goals that prioritize progress and personal growth over perfection. Focus on continuous improvement rather than striving for flawless outcomes, and celebrate your efforts and accomplishments along the way.

Embrace Collaboration over Competition

Shift your mindset from competition to collaboration, recognizing that success is not a zero-sum game. Instead of viewing peers as rivals, see them as potential collaborators, mentors, or sources of inspiration. Embrace opportunities to learn from others and leverage their strengths to complement your own.

Focus on Your Unique Path

Focus on your unique strengths, values, and interests, rather than comparing yourself to others. Embrace your individuality and pursue goals that align with your authentic self, rather than trying to conform to external expectations or standards of success.

Foster a Growth Mindset

Cultivate a growth mindset that views challenges and setbacks as opportunities for learning and growth. Embrace the process of experimentation, iteration, and adaptation, recognizing that failure is a natural part of the journey towards mastery and innovation.

Set Boundaries and Prioritize Self-Care

Set boundaries to protect your time, energy, and well-being in competitive environments. Prioritize self-care activities such as exercise, meditation, or hobbies that recharge your creative spirit and foster resilience in the face of pressure or stress.

Overcoming Perfectionism Paralysis

Perfectionism paralysis occurs when the fear of failure or judgment prevents individuals from taking action on their goals or pursuing new opportunities. Here are some strategies for overcoming perfectionism paralysis:

Take Imperfect Action

Take imperfect action by embracing the concept of "good enough" rather than waiting for perfect conditions or outcomes. Recognize that perfection is subjective and that progress is more important than perfection. Start small, take risks, and learn from mistakes along the way.

Seek Feedback and Support

Seek feedback and support from trusted peers, mentors, or collaborators who can offer constructive criticism and encouragement. Share your ideas and projects openly with others, inviting feedback and perspectives that can help you grow and improve.

Reframe Failure as Learning Opportunity

Reframe failure as a natural and necessary part of the learning process. Embrace setbacks as opportunities for growth and discovery, rather than evidence of personal inadequacy. Adopt a growth mindset that views challenges as stepping stones to success, rather than insurmountable obstacles.

Conclusion

Navigating perfectionism in competitive environments requires a combination of self-awareness, self-compassion, and boundary-setting. By practicing self-compassion, setting realistic expectations, embracing collaboration over competition, focusing on your unique path, fostering a growth mindset, and prioritizing self-care, you can overcome perfectionism tendencies and thrive in competitive fields.

In the next chapter, we'll explore strategies for overcoming procrastination burnout and rekindling motivation and creativity in times of exhaustion or overwhelm. Through intentional action and a commitment to personal growth, you can cultivate a healthier relationship with perfectionism and competition, allowing you to pursue your goals with confidence, resilience, and authenticity.

CHAPTER TWENTY
OVERCOMING PROCRASTINATION BURNOUT
Focus: This Is Exhausting…

Procrastination burnout is a common phenomenon that occurs when prolonged periods of procrastination lead to feelings of exhaustion, overwhelm, and diminished motivation. In this chapter, we'll explore the causes and consequences of procrastination burnout, and provide strategies for overcoming it to rekindle motivation and creativity.

Understanding Procrastination Burnout

Procrastination burnout occurs when the stress and anxiety associated with procrastination become overwhelming, leading to mental, emotional, and physical exhaustion. Prolonged periods of procrastination can erode motivation, increase stress levels, and impair cognitive function, making it difficult to focus, make decisions, or take action.

Causes of Procrastination Burnout

Procrastination burnout can be caused by various factors, including:

- **Perfectionism:** The relentless pursuit of perfection can lead to analysis paralysis and decision fatigue, draining energy and motivation over time.

- **Overwhelm:** Feeling overwhelmed by the sheer volume or complexity of tasks can lead to procrastination as a coping mechanism, but it can also exacerbate feelings of stress and burnout.

- **Lack of Self-Compassion:** Harsh self-criticism and negative self-talk can undermine self-confidence and contribute to procrastination burnout by eroding resilience and motivation.

Consequences of Procrastination Burnout

Procrastination burnout can have profound consequences on mental health, well-being, and productivity, including:

- **Decreased Motivation:** Procrastination burnout can sap motivation and enthusiasm for creative endeavors, making it difficult to muster the energy to start or complete tasks.

- **Increased Stress:** Prolonged periods of procrastination can increase stress levels, leading to heightened anxiety, irritability, and difficulty coping with daily challenges.

- **Impaired Performance:** Procrastination burnout can impair cognitive function and decision-making abilities, leading to decreased productivity and performance.

Strategies for Overcoming Procrastination Burnout

Overcoming procrastination burnout requires a combination of self-care, self-compassion, and proactive action. Here are some strategies for rekindling motivation and creativity in times of procrastination burnout:

Prioritize Self-Care

Prioritize self-care activities such as exercise, meditation, or hobbies that recharge your energy and reduce stress levels. Take regular breaks throughout the day to rest and rejuvenate, allowing yourself to step away from work and engage in activities that bring you joy and relaxation.

Break Tasks into Smaller Steps

Break tasks into smaller, more manageable steps to reduce overwhelm and make progress feel more attainable. Focus on completing one small task at a time, celebrating each accomplishment along the way. By breaking tasks into smaller chunks, you can overcome inertia and build momentum towards your goals.

Set Realistic Goals and Expectations

Set realistic, achievable goals that align with your priorities and values. Avoid setting overly ambitious or perfectionistic goals that set you up for failure and disappointment. Instead, focus on making incremental progress and celebrating small victories along the way.

Practice Self-Compassion

Practice self-compassion by treating yourself with kindness and understanding, especially during times of procrastination burnout. Acknowledge the challenges you're facing and remind yourself that it's okay to take breaks and ask for support when needed. Treat yourself with the same level of care and compassion you would offer to a friend in a similar situation.

Seek Support and Accountability

Seek support and accountability from trusted friends, family members, or mentors who can offer encouragement, guidance, and perspective. Share your struggles openly with others, allowing yourself to receive support and validation without judgment or criticism. Having someone to hold you accountable can help keep you motivated and on track towards your goals.

Reevaluate Your Priorities

Take time to reevaluate your priorities and commitments, making adjustments as needed to align with your values and goals. Identify tasks or obligations that no longer serve you or contribute to your overall well-being, and consider letting go of them to create space for activities that bring you joy and fulfillment.

Cultivate Mindfulness and Presence

Cultivate mindfulness and presence in your daily life, allowing yourself to fully engage in the present moment without judgment or distraction. Practice mindfulness meditation or deep breathing exercises to calm your mind and body, reducing stress and enhancing focus and clarity

Overcoming Procrastination Burnout

Procrastination burnout can be a challenging obstacle to overcome, but with self-awareness, self-compassion, and proactive action, it is possible to rekindle motivation and creativity. By prioritizing self-care, setting realistic goals and expectations, practicing self-compassion, seeking support and accountability, reevaluating priorities, and cultivating mindfulness and presence, you can overcome procrastination burnout and reignite your passion for creative pursuits.

In the next chapter, we'll explore the power of saying no and setting boundaries to protect your time, energy, and creative focus. Through intentional action and a commitment to self-care and personal growth, you can overcome procrastination burnout and thrive as a creator.

CHAPTER TWENTY-ONE
THE POWER OF SAYING NO
Focus: Know Your Limits

In a world filled with endless opportunities and demands on our time and energy, learning to say no is a powerful skill that can protect our well-being, foster productivity, and preserve our creative focus. In this chapter, we'll explore the importance of setting boundaries and prioritizing our commitments, and provide strategies for saying no gracefully and assertively.

Understanding the Importance of Saying No

Saying no is not about being selfish or uncooperative; it's about honoring our own needs, values, and priorities. By saying no to commitments that do not align with our goals or values, we create space for activities that bring us joy, fulfillment, and meaning. Saying no allows us to protect our time, energy, and creative focus, enabling us to pursue our passions and goals with clarity and purpose.

The Cost of Saying Yes to Everything

When we say yes to every request or opportunity that comes our way, we risk spreading ourselves too thin and neglecting our own needs and priorities. Overcommitment can lead to stress, burnout, and resentment, as we struggle to meet unrealistic expectations and juggle competing demands on our time and energy. By learning to say no strategically, we can avoid overcommitment and focus on what truly matters to us.

Strategies for Saying No Gracefully

Saying no can be challenging, especially for people-pleasers or those who fear conflict or rejection. However, with practice and assertiveness, saying no can become a liberating act of self-care and empowerment. Here are some strategies for saying no gracefully:

Be Clear and Direct

When saying no, be clear and direct about your decision, avoiding ambiguity or mixed messages. Clearly communicate your reasons for declining the request, but do so with kindness and respect. Express gratitude for the opportunity, but firmly assert your decision to decline.

Offer Alternatives

If possible, offer alternatives or compromises that demonstrate your willingness to help in other ways. Suggest alternative solutions or resources that may meet the requester's needs without requiring your direct involvement. By offering alternatives, you can soften the impact of your refusal and maintain goodwill in the relationship.

Practice Assertiveness

Practice assertiveness techniques such as using "I" statements, maintaining eye contact, and speaking with confidence and conviction. Assertiveness allows you to communicate your boundaries and priorities effectively while respecting the needs and feelings of others. Remember that it's okay to prioritize your own well-being and say no when necessary.

Set Boundaries

Establish clear boundaries around your time, energy, and resources, and communicate them assertively to others. Explain what you are willing and able to do, and be firm in enforcing your boundaries when they are tested. Setting boundaries is essential for protecting your well-being and maintaining a healthy work-life balance.

Overcoming Guilt and FOMO

One of the biggest obstacles to saying no is the fear of missing out (FOMO) or feeling guilty for letting others down. However, it's important to recognize that saying no is not a reflection of your worth or value as a person. It's okay to prioritize your own needs and well-being, even if it means disappointing others temporarily. Remember that saying no allows you to show up more fully and authentically in the areas of your life that matter most to you.

Conclusion

Learning to say no is a valuable skill that can empower us to prioritize our own needs and values, protect our time and energy, and pursue our passions and goals with clarity and purpose. By being clear and direct, offering alternatives, practicing assertiveness, and setting boundaries, we can say no gracefully and assertively, without sacrificing our relationships or self-esteem.

In the next chapter, we'll explore the importance of embracing flexibility and adaptability in the face of change and uncertainty. Through intentional action and a commitment to self-care and personal growth, we can create a life that aligns with our values and brings us joy, fulfillment, and meaning.

CHAPTER TWENTY-TWO
EMBRACING FLEXIBILITY AND ADAPTABILITY
Focus: Accept Change and Uncertainty

In a world characterized by constant change and uncertainty, embracing flexibility and adaptability is essential for navigating life's challenges and seizing opportunities for growth and innovation. In this chapter, we'll explore the importance of flexibility and adaptability in various aspects of life, and provide strategies for cultivating these qualities to thrive in an ever-changing world.

Understanding Flexibility and Adaptability

Flexibility and adaptability are closely related but distinct qualities that enable individuals to respond effectively to change and adversity. While flexibility involves being open to new ideas, perspectives, and experiences, adaptability goes a step further by actively adjusting to changing circumstances and learning from them.

The Importance of Flexibility and Adaptability

In today's fast-paced world, the ability to adapt to change is more important than ever. Whether facing personal challenges, professional transitions, or global crises, individuals who possess flexibility and adaptability are better equipped to navigate uncertainty, overcome obstacles, and thrive in dynamic environments.

Cultivating Flexibility and Adaptability

Flexibility and adaptability are qualities that can be cultivated through self-awareness, resilience, and intentional action. Here are some strategies for cultivating flexibility and adaptability in various aspects of life:

Embrace Change and Uncertainty

Embrace change and uncertainty as natural and inevitable parts of the human experience. Instead of resisting or fearing change, adopt a mindset of curiosity and exploration, viewing new challenges as opportunities for growth and learning. By reframing change as a catalyst for personal and professional development, you can embrace uncertainty with confidence and resilience.

Adjust Goals and Strategies as Needed

Be willing to adjust your goals and strategies in response to changing circumstances or unexpected obstacles. Flexibility involves being open to alternative paths and solutions, even if they diverge from your original plans. By remaining adaptable and willing to pivot when necessary, you can navigate detours and setbacks with grace and determination.

Find Opportunity in Adversity

Find opportunity in adversity by reframing challenges as opportunities for innovation and creativity. Instead of viewing setbacks as failures, see them as valuable learning experiences that can fuel personal growth and resilience. Cultivate a mindset of optimism and resilience, focusing on solutions rather than dwelling on problems.

Flexibility and Adaptability in Personal Life

Flexibility and adaptability are essential qualities for navigating the complexities of personal relationships, managing life transitions, and maintaining emotional well-being. Here are some strategies for cultivating flexibility and adaptability in your personal life:

Practice Open Communication

Practice open communication and active listening in your personal relationships, allowing space for honest dialogue and mutual understanding. Be willing to compromise and negotiate with others, recognizing that flexibility is key to resolving conflicts and building strong, resilient relationships.

Embrace Life Transitions

Embrace life transitions such as career changes, relocations, or relationship shifts as opportunities for growth and self-discovery. Instead of clinging to the familiar or resisting change, approach transitions with curiosity and optimism, trusting in your ability to adapt and thrive in new environments.

Prioritize Self-Care and Well-Being

Prioritize self-care and well-being to maintain resilience and balance in your personal life. Practice self-care activities such as exercise, mindfulness, and creative expression to recharge your energy and reduce stress levels. Cultivate healthy habits and boundaries that support your physical, emotional, and mental well-being.

Flexibility and Adaptability in Professional Life

Flexibility and adaptability are also critical for success in the workplace, where rapid technological advancements, economic fluctuations, and shifting market demands require agility and innovation. Here are some strategies for cultivating flexibility and adaptability in your professional life:

Embrace Lifelong Learning

Embrace lifelong learning and professional development to stay relevant and adaptable in a rapidly changing job market. Seek opportunities for skill-building, continuing education, and networking to expand your knowledge and expertise. Be proactive in seeking out new challenges and opportunities for growth within your career field.

Foster Collaboration and Innovation

Foster a culture of collaboration and innovation in your workplace, encouraging openness to new ideas and perspectives. Create space for creative brainstorming, experimentation, and risk-taking, recognizing that innovation often arises from diverse perspectives and collaborative efforts.

Stay Agile and Resilient

Stay agile and resilient in the face of organizational changes or unexpected challenges. Adapt quickly to shifting priorities, market trends, or technological advancements, and be willing to pivot your strategies or approaches as needed. Cultivate a mindset of resilience and resourcefulness, focusing on solutions rather than dwelling on obstacles.

Overcoming Resistance to Change

Resistance to change is a common barrier to flexibility and adaptability, rooted in fear of the unknown or attachment to the status quo. Here are some strategies for overcoming resistance to change and embracing flexibility and adaptability:

Cultivate a Growth Mindset

Cultivate a growth mindset that views challenges and setbacks as opportunities for learning and growth. Embrace change as a natural and necessary part of the human experience, recognizing that adaptation and innovation are essential for personal and professional development.

Practice Self-Compassion

Practice self-compassion and kindness towards yourself during times of change or transition. Be patient and gentle with yourself as you navigate uncertainty, recognizing that change can be challenging and uncomfortable. Treat yourself with the same level of understanding and support you would offer to a friend in a similar situation.

Seek Support and Guidance

Seek support and guidance from mentors, peers, or trusted advisors who can offer perspective and encouragement during times of change. Lean on your support network for emotional support and practical advice, allowing yourself to receive help without judgment or shame.

Conclusion

Flexibility and adaptability are essential qualities for navigating the complexities of life and thriving in an ever-changing world. By embracing change and uncertainty, adjusting goals and strategies as needed, and finding opportunity in adversity, you can cultivate flexibility and adaptability in both your personal and professional life. Through intentional action and a commitment to lifelong learning and growth, you can develop the resilience and agility needed to navigate life's challenges with confidence and grace.

In the next chapter, we'll explore the importance of creating a procrastination-proof lifestyle and maintaining consistency and persistence in pursuit of your goals.

CHAPTER TWENTY-THREE
CREATING A PROCRASTINATION-PROOF LIFESTYLE
Focus: This Is Your New Normal

In a world filled with distractions and competing priorities, creating a procrastination-proof lifestyle is essential for achieving our goals and living with intention. In this chapter, we'll explore strategies for establishing healthy habits, cultivating a supportive environment, and maintaining consistency and persistence in pursuit of our aspirations.

Establishing Healthy Habits

Healthy habits form the foundation of a procrastination-proof lifestyle, providing structure, routine, and discipline to our daily lives. Here are some key habits to cultivate:

Prioritize Self-Care

Prioritize self-care activities such as exercise, mindfulness, and adequate sleep to recharge your energy and reduce stress levels. Make time for activities that bring you joy and fulfillment, and listen to your body's signals for rest and relaxation.

Set Clear Goals

Set clear, specific goals that align with your values and priorities. Break larger goals down into smaller, more manageable tasks, and create a plan of action to achieve them. By setting clear goals and deadlines, you can maintain focus and motivation to overcome procrastination.

Establish Daily Routines

Establish daily routines and rituals to create structure and consistency in your life. Set aside dedicated time each day for work, leisure, and self-care activities, and stick to your schedule as much as possible. Consistent routines can help reduce decision fatigue and increase productivity.

Practice Time Management

Practice effective time management techniques such as prioritization, time-blocking, and goal-setting to maximize productivity and minimize procrastination. Use tools such as calendars, to-do lists, and productivity apps to organize your tasks and stay on track.

Cultivating a Supportive Environment

Creating a supportive environment is crucial for minimizing distractions and staying focused on your goals. Here are some ways to cultivate a supportive environment:

Minimize Distractions

Identify and eliminate distractions in your environment that may contribute to procrastination. Create a dedicated workspace that is free from clutter and interruptions, and use tools such as website blockers or noise-cancelling headphones to minimize distractions while working.

Surround Yourself with Positivity

Surround yourself with positive influences and like-minded individuals who support your goals and aspirations. Seek out mentors, peers, or accountability partners who can offer encouragement, guidance, and perspective during times of challenge or uncertainty.

Set Boundaries

Set clear boundaries around your time, energy, and resources, and communicate them assertively to others. Learn to say no to requests or commitments that do not align with your goals or priorities, and prioritize activities that contribute to your overall well-being and fulfillment.

Create Accountability Systems

Create accountability systems to help you stay on track towards your goals and hold yourself accountable for your actions. Share your goals and progress with others, and enlist their support in keeping you motivated and focused. Consider joining a mastermind group, hiring a coach, or using apps that track your progress and provide feedback.

Maintaining Consistency and Persistence

Consistency and persistence are key to overcoming procrastination and achieving long-term success. Here are some strategies for maintaining consistency and persistence in pursuit of your goals:

Focus on Progress, Not Perfection

Focus on making progress towards your goals, rather than striving for perfection. Embrace the concept of "good enough" and celebrate small victories along the way. Remember that consistent effort and incremental improvement are more important than achieving flawless results.

Stay Committed to Your Vision

Stay committed to your vision and remind yourself of your reasons for pursuing your goals. Visualize your desired outcomes and the benefits they will bring to your life, and use this vision to stay motivated and focused during challenging times.

Practice Resilience

Practice resilience by bouncing back from setbacks and failures with grace and determination. View setbacks as learning opportunities rather than insurmountable obstacles, and use them to course-correct and refine your approach. Cultivate a growth mindset that embraces challenges as opportunities for growth and development.

Celebrate Your Progress

Celebrate your progress and achievements along the way, no matter how small. Acknowledge your efforts and accomplishments, and take time to reflect on how far you've come. Celebrating progress boosts motivation and reinforces positive habits, making it easier to stay consistent and persistent in pursuit of your goals.

Conclusion

Creating a procrastination-proof lifestyle requires cultivating healthy habits, cultivating a supportive environment, and maintaining consistency and persistence in pursuit of our goals. By prioritizing self-care, setting clear goals, establishing daily routines, practicing time management, minimizing distractions, surrounding ourselves with positivity, setting boundaries, creating accountability systems, focusing on progress, staying committed to our vision, practicing resilience, and celebrating progress, we can overcome procrastination and achieve our aspirations with confidence and determination.

In the next chapter, we'll explore strategies for overcoming setbacks and relapses, and building resilience in the face of adversity. Through intentional action and a commitment to personal growth, we can create a life that reflects our values and brings us joy, fulfillment, and meaning.

CHAPTER TWENTY-FOUR
OVERCOMING SETBACKS AND RELAPSES
Focus: Focus On Your Progress

Setbacks and relapses are inevitable parts of any journey toward personal growth and achievement. In this chapter, we'll explore the nature of setbacks and relapses, their impact on our progress, and strategies for overcoming them with resilience and determination.

Understanding Setbacks and Relapses

Setbacks and relapses are temporary disruptions or regressions in our progress toward our goals. They can occur for a variety of reasons, including unforeseen challenges, mistakes, or lapses in motivation or discipline. Setbacks and relapses are natural and normal parts of the learning process, and they provide valuable opportunities for growth and self-reflection.

Types of Setbacks

- **External Challenges:** Unexpected obstacles or setbacks outside of our control, such as financial difficulties, health issues, or changes in circumstances.

- **Internal Struggles:** Personal challenges or barriers that arise from within, such as self-doubt, fear of failure, or negative self-talk.

- **Mistakes and Failures:** Errors in judgment or execution that lead to setbacks or setbacks, such as missed deadlines, poor decisions, or unsuccessful attempts.

Impact of Setbacks and Relapses

Setbacks and relapses can have a significant impact on our progress and well-being, including:

- **Emotional Distress:** Feelings of frustration, disappointment, or shame may arise in response to setbacks or relapses, leading to decreased motivation and self-esteem.

- **Loss of Momentum:** Setbacks and relapses can disrupt our momentum and derail our progress toward our goals, making it difficult to regain traction and move forward.

- **Self-Doubt:** Setbacks and relapses may trigger self-doubt or negative self-talk, causing us to question our abilities or worthiness of success.

Strategies for Overcoming Setbacks and Relapses

While setbacks and relapses can be challenging, they also present opportunities for growth, resilience, and learning. Here are some strategies for overcoming setbacks and relapses with grace and determination:

Practice Self-Compassion

Practice self-compassion and kindness toward yourself during times of difficulty or setback. Treat yourself with the same level of understanding and support you would offer to a friend in a similar situation. Remember that setbacks are a natural part of the journey toward success, and they do not define your worth or potential.

Learn from Mistakes

View setbacks and relapses as valuable learning opportunities rather than failures. Take time to reflect on what went wrong and identify lessons learned from the experience. Use this knowledge to adjust your approach, refine your strategies, and make informed decisions moving forward.

Reframe Setbacks as Learning Opportunities

Reframe setbacks as opportunities for growth and development. Instead of dwelling on the negative aspects of the situation, focus on what you can learn from it and how you can use this knowledge to improve in the future. Embrace a growth mindset that recognizes challenges as stepping stones to success.

Seek Support and Encouragement

Seek support and encouragement from trusted friends, family members, or mentors who can offer perspective, guidance, and encouragement during times of setback or relapse. Share your struggles openly with others, and allow yourself to receive support and validation without judgment or criticism.

Stay Committed to Your Goals

Stay committed to your goals and vision, even in the face of setbacks and challenges. Use setbacks as fuel for your determination and motivation, and remind yourself of the reasons why you started your journey in the first place. Visualize your desired outcomes and the benefits they will bring to your life, and use this vision to stay focused and resilient.

Take Action Toward Recovery

Take proactive steps toward recovery and regaining momentum after a setback or relapse. Break tasks down into smaller, more manageable steps, and take incremental actions toward your goals. Celebrate small victories along the way, and use each success as motivation to keep moving forward.

Conclusion

Setbacks and relapses are inevitable parts of any journey toward personal growth and achievement. While they can be challenging and disheartening, setbacks also present opportunities for growth, resilience, and learning. By practicing self-compassion, learning from mistakes, reframing setbacks as learning opportunities, seeking support and encouragement, staying committed to your goals, and taking proactive action toward recovery, you can overcome setbacks and relapses with grace and determination.

In the next chapter, we'll explore the importance of cultivating gratitude and positivity as a means of fostering resilience and well-being. Through intentional action and a commitment to personal growth, you can navigate setbacks with confidence and emerge stronger and more resilient than ever before.

CHAPTER TWENTY-FIVE
CULTIVATING GRATITUDE AND POSITIVITY
Focus: Good Feelings; Good Health; Good Life

In a world filled with challenges and uncertainties, cultivating gratitude and positivity can serve as powerful tools for fostering resilience, well-being, and overall happiness. In this chapter, we'll explore the importance of gratitude and positivity, their benefits for mental and emotional health, and practical strategies for incorporating them into our daily lives.

Understanding Gratitude and Positivity

Gratitude is the practice of recognizing and appreciating the good things in our lives, both big and small. It involves acknowledging the blessings, kindness, and abundance that surround us, even in difficult times. Positivity, on the other hand, is the practice of maintaining an optimistic and hopeful outlook, focusing on the bright side of life and finding joy in everyday moments.

The Power of Gratitude and Positivity

Gratitude and positivity have been linked to numerous benefits for mental, emotional, and physical health. Research has shown that practicing gratitude can improve mood, enhance resilience, and reduce symptoms of depression and anxiety. Similarly, cultivating a positive outlook can lead to greater life satisfaction, increased motivation, and improved overall well-being.

Benefits of Cultivating Gratitude and Positivity

Cultivating gratitude and positivity offers a wide range of benefits, including:

- **Improved Mental Health:** Gratitude and positivity have been shown to reduce symptoms of depression and anxiety, increase feelings of happiness and life satisfaction, and enhance overall psychological well-being.

- **Enhanced Resilience:** Practicing gratitude and positivity can help build resilience by fostering a mindset of optimism and hopefulness, even in the face of adversity or challenges.

- **Better Relationships:** Expressing gratitude and positivity toward others can strengthen relationships, foster connection and empathy, and enhance overall satisfaction in interpersonal interactions.

- **Physical Health Benefits:** Gratitude and positivity have been associated with improved physical health outcomes, including better sleep, reduced inflammation, and increased immune function.

Strategies for Cultivating Gratitude and Positivity

Incorporating gratitude and positivity into our daily lives doesn't have to be complicated or time-consuming. Here are some simple yet effective strategies for cultivating gratitude and positivity:

Keep a Gratitude Journal

Take a few minutes each day to write down three things you're grateful for. These can be big or small, from a delicious meal to a supportive friend or a beautiful sunset. Keeping a gratitude journal helps shift your focus from what's wrong to what's going right in your life.

Practice Mindfulness

Engage in mindfulness practices such as meditation, deep breathing, or mindful walking to cultivate present-moment awareness and appreciation. Mindfulness allows you to savor the simple joys of life and connect more deeply with the present moment.

Express Appreciation

Express gratitude and appreciation toward others by offering sincere compliments, thank-you notes, or acts of kindness. Letting others know you appreciate them not only strengthens your relationships but also fosters a sense of connection and belonging.

Reframe Negative Thoughts

Challenge negative thoughts and beliefs by reframing them in a more positive light. Instead of focusing on what's going wrong, look for silver linings or opportunities for growth in difficult situations. Cultivating a positive outlook can help you find hope and resilience even in challenging times.

Practice Self-Compassion

Practice self-compassion by treating yourself with kindness and understanding, especially during times of difficulty or struggle. Be gentle with yourself when things don't go as planned, and remind yourself of your inherent worth and value.

Incorporating Gratitude and Positivity into Daily Life

Make gratitude and positivity a regular part of your daily routine by incorporating them into your habits and rituals. Here are some ways to integrate gratitude and positivity into your daily life:

Start and End Your Day with Gratitude

Begin each day by reflecting on three things you're grateful for, and end each day by noting three positive experiences or moments that brought you joy. This practice helps set a positive tone for the day ahead and promotes restful sleep and relaxation at night.

Practice Gratitude During Meals

Before meals, take a moment to pause and express gratitude for the food you're about to eat, as well as the people who contributed to its preparation. Cultivating gratitude during meals can enhance your enjoyment of food and foster a sense of connection and appreciation for the nourishment it provides.

Create a Gratitude Ritual

Create a gratitude ritual that you can perform regularly, such as writing thank-you notes, keeping a gratitude jar, or practicing a gratitude meditation. Consistently engaging in these rituals reinforces the habit of gratitude and encourages a positive outlook on life.

Conclusion

Cultivating gratitude and positivity is a powerful practice that can enhance our mental, emotional, and physical well-being, and enrich our overall quality of life. By recognizing and appreciating the blessings in our lives, maintaining an optimistic and hopeful outlook, and incorporating simple gratitude and positivity practices into our daily routines, we can experience greater happiness, resilience, and fulfillment.

In the next chapter, we'll explore the journey of self-improvement and the importance of embracing growth and change as we strive to become the best versions of ourselves. Through intentional action and a commitment to personal growth, we can create a life that reflects our values and brings us joy, meaning, and purpose.

CHAPTER TWENTY-SIX
EMBRACING THE JOURNEY OF SELF-IMPROVEMENT
Focus: Becoming Your Best You

The journey of self-improvement is a transformative process that involves personal growth, learning, and development. In this chapter, we'll explore the importance of embracing self-improvement, the benefits it brings to our lives, and practical strategies for fostering growth and change.

Understanding Self-Improvement

Self-improvement is the ongoing process of enhancing our knowledge, skills, habits, and attitudes to become the best versions of ourselves. It involves setting goals, overcoming obstacles, and continuously striving for personal growth and fulfillment. Self-improvement encompasses various areas of life, including physical, mental, emotional, and spiritual well-being.

The Importance of Self-Improvement

Self-improvement is essential for living a fulfilling and meaningful life. It allows us to expand our potential, overcome limitations, and achieve our goals and aspirations. By embracing self-improvement, we can enhance our quality of life, increase our resilience and adaptability, and cultivate a sense of purpose and fulfillment.

Benefits of Self-Improvement

Embracing self-improvement offers a wide range of benefits for our overall well-being and success. Some of the key benefits include:

- **Personal Growth:** Self-improvement fosters personal growth and development, allowing us to become more self-aware, confident, and resilient individuals.

- **Enhanced Skills and Abilities:** Engaging in self-improvement activities helps us acquire new skills, knowledge, and competencies that enable us to excel in various areas of life.

- **Increased Happiness and Fulfillment:** Pursuing self-improvement activities that align with our values and interests can lead to greater happiness, fulfillment, and life satisfaction.

- **Improved Relationships:** By working on ourselves, we become better equipped to navigate relationships and communicate effectively with others, leading to stronger, more meaningful connections.

Strategies for Embracing Self-Improvement

Embracing self-improvement requires commitment, dedication, and a willingness to step out of our comfort zones. Here are some practical strategies for fostering growth and change:

Set Clear Goals

Identify specific areas of your life that you would like to improve and set clear, achievable goals for yourself. Break larger goals down into smaller, more manageable steps, and create a plan of action to help you achieve them. Having clear goals provides direction and motivation for your self-improvement journey.

Cultivate a Growth Mindset

Adopt a growth mindset that embraces challenges, failures, and setbacks as opportunities for learning and growth. Believe in your ability to develop and improve over time, and view obstacles as temporary roadblocks on the path to success. Cultivating a growth mindset fosters resilience, creativity, and innovation.

Practice Self-Reflection

Regularly engage in self-reflection to assess your progress, strengths, and areas for improvement. Set aside time to journal, meditate, or simply sit quietly and reflect on your thoughts, feelings, and experiences. Self-reflection allows you to gain insight into yourself and your life, identify patterns and trends, and make informed decisions about your personal growth.

Step Out of Your Comfort Zone

Challenge yourself to step out of your comfort zone and try new things that stretch your abilities and expand your horizons. Whether it's learning a new skill, taking on a new hobby, or pursuing a new career path, embracing discomfort is essential for growth and self-discovery. Embrace uncertainty and embrace the opportunity to learn and grow from your experiences.

Seek Feedback and Support

Seek feedback and support from others who can offer guidance, encouragement, and constructive criticism on your self-improvement journey. Surround yourself with mentors, coaches, and peers who inspire and challenge you to reach your full potential. Be open to receiving feedback with humility and gratitude, and use it as an opportunity for growth and development.

Conclusion

Embracing the journey of self-improvement is a transformative process that allows us to become the best versions of ourselves. By setting clear goals, cultivating a growth mindset, practicing self-reflection, stepping out of our comfort zones, and seeking feedback and support, we can foster personal growth, resilience, and fulfillment in our lives. Through intentional action and a commitment to lifelong learning and growth, we can create a life that reflects our values and aspirations, and brings us joy, meaning, and purpose.

In the next chapter, we'll explore the importance of paying it forward and supporting others in their journey of self-improvement. Through acts of kindness, generosity, and mentorship, we can inspire and empower others to reach their full potential and create positive change in the world.

CHAPTER TWENTY-SEVEN
PAYING IT FORWARD
Focus: Helping Others Helps You

Paying it forward is a concept that involves performing acts of kindness or generosity towards others with the expectation that they will do the same for someone else, creating a ripple effect of goodwill and positive change. In this chapter, we'll explore the importance of paying it forward, its benefits for both the giver and the receiver, and practical ways to incorporate it into our daily lives.

Understanding Paying It Forward

Paying it forward is rooted in the belief that small acts of kindness have the power to make a big difference in the world. Whether it's offering a helping hand to someone in need, lending a listening ear to a friend in distress, or simply spreading joy and positivity through random acts of kindness, paying it forward allows us to contribute to the well-being of others and create a ripple effect of positivity and compassion.

The Power of Paying It Forward

Paying it forward has the power to create a positive impact on both individuals and communities. By practicing kindness and generosity, we not only uplift others and make their lives a little brighter, but we also experience a sense of fulfillment, connection, and purpose. Paying it forward strengthens social bonds, fosters empathy and compassion, and builds a sense of community and belonging.

Benefits of Paying It Forward

Engaging in acts of kindness and generosity offers a wide range of benefits for both the giver and the receiver. Some of the key benefits include:

- **Increased Happiness:** Performing acts of kindness activates the brain's reward centers, leading to feelings of happiness and fulfillment. Giving to others boosts our mood and sense of well-being, leading to greater overall happiness and life satisfaction.

- **Improved Mental Health:** Practicing kindness and generosity has been linked to reduced stress, anxiety, and depression. Acts of kindness promote positive emotions and feelings of connection, which contribute to improved mental and emotional well-being.

- **Enhanced Social Connection:** Paying it forward strengthens social bonds and fosters a sense of connection and belonging within communities. Acts of kindness create opportunities for meaningful interactions and shared experiences, leading to stronger, more supportive relationships.

- **Positive Ripple Effect:** Acts of kindness have a ripple effect, inspiring others to pay it forward and create positive change in their own lives and communities. By spreading kindness and generosity, we contribute to a more compassionate and caring world.

Practical Ways to Pay It Forward

Incorporating paying it forward into our daily lives doesn't have to be complicated or time-consuming. Here are some simple yet impactful ways to practice kindness and generosity:

Random Acts of Kindness

Perform random acts of kindness for strangers, friends, or loved ones. Whether it's paying for someone's coffee, holding the door open for a stranger, or leaving an encouraging note for a coworker, small gestures of kindness can brighten someone's day and inspire them to pay it forward.

Volunteer Your Time

Volunteer your time and talents to support causes and organizations that are meaningful to you. Whether it's volunteering at a local soup kitchen, mentoring a child, or participating in a community clean-up project, giving back to your community fosters a sense of connection and purpose.

Practice Active Listening

Practice active listening by offering your full attention and support to others in need. Take the time to listen empathetically to their concerns, validate their feelings, and offer encouragement and support. Sometimes, the simple act of being present and supportive can make a world of difference to someone in need.

Spread Positivity Online

Spread positivity and kindness on social media by sharing uplifting messages, words of encouragement, or acts of kindness. Use your platform to inspire and uplift others, and create a positive online community that promotes kindness, empathy, and connection.

Express Gratitude

Express gratitude and appreciation toward others for their kindness and generosity. Take the time to thank people for their acts of kindness, whether it's with a heartfelt thank-you note, a verbal expression of gratitude, or a small token of appreciation. Acknowledging and appreciating the kindness of others reinforces the cycle of giving and receiving.

Conclusion

Paying it forward is a powerful practice that allows us to spread kindness, generosity, and compassion to others, creating a ripple effect of positivity and goodwill in the world. By engaging in acts of kindness, we not only uplift others and make a positive impact on their lives, but we also experience greater happiness, fulfillment, and connection ourselves. Through simple acts of kindness, we can inspire others to do the same and create a more compassionate and caring world for all.

In the next chapter, we'll explore the importance of living a life of purpose and fulfillment, and the role of self-improvement in achieving our highest aspirations. Through intentional action and a commitment to making a difference, we can create positive change in the world and leave a lasting legacy of kindness and compassion.

CHAPTER TWENTY-EIGHT
LIVING A LIFE OF PURPOSE AND FULFILLMENT
Focus: This Is An Ongoing Journey

Living a life of purpose and fulfillment is a journey of self-discovery, growth, and contribution to the world. In this chapter, we'll explore the importance of finding our purpose, the benefits of living with intention, and practical strategies for aligning our actions with our values to create a life of meaning and fulfillment.

Understanding Purpose and Fulfillment

Purpose is the sense of direction and meaning that drives our actions and choices in life. It gives us a reason to wake up in the morning, fuels our passions and interests, and guides us towards our highest aspirations. Fulfillment, on the other hand, is the deep sense of satisfaction and contentment that arises from living in alignment with our values and making a positive impact on the world.

The Importance of Purpose and Fulfillment

Having a sense of purpose and fulfillment is essential for our overall well-being and happiness. Research has shown that people who live with a sense of purpose tend to experience greater resilience, motivation, and life satisfaction. They are more likely to overcome challenges, pursue their goals with determination, and find meaning and fulfillment in their lives.

Benefits of Living with Purpose and Fulfillment

Living with purpose and fulfillment offers a wide range of benefits for our mental, emotional, and physical well-being. Some of the key benefits include:

- **Greater Happiness:** Living a life aligned with our values and passions leads to greater overall happiness and life satisfaction. When we know what we stand for and pursue our goals with intention, we experience a deep sense of fulfillment and contentment.

- **Increased Resilience:** Having a sense of purpose gives us the strength and motivation to persevere through challenges and setbacks. When we have a clear sense of direction and meaning in life, we are better able to navigate obstacles and overcome adversity.

- **Improved Mental Health:** Living with purpose and fulfillment has been linked to reduced symptoms of depression, anxiety, and stress. When we live in alignment with our values and passions, we experience greater emotional well-being and psychological resilience.

- **Enhanced Relationships:** When we live with purpose and fulfillment, we are better able to connect with others authentically and form meaningful relationships. Our sense of purpose and fulfillment enhances our ability to empathize, communicate, and collaborate with others, leading to deeper, more fulfilling connections.

Strategies for Living with Purpose and Fulfillment

Living with purpose and fulfillment requires introspection, self-awareness, and intentional action. Here are some practical strategies for aligning your life with your values and passions:

Clarify Your Values and Passions

Take the time to reflect on your values, passions, and priorities in life. What matters most to you? What brings you joy, fulfillment, and a sense of meaning? Clarifying your values and passions provides a foundation for living with purpose and aligning your actions with what truly matters to you.

Set Meaningful Goals

Set goals that are aligned with your values, passions, and aspirations. Consider what you want to achieve in different areas of your life, such as career, relationships, health, and personal growth. Set SMART goals (Specific, Measurable, Achievable, Relevant, and Time-bound) that challenge and inspire you to become the best version of yourself.

Take Purposeful Action

Take intentional action towards your goals and aspirations. Break larger goals down into smaller, more manageable steps, and create a plan of action to help you achieve them. Focus on activities that bring you closer to your goals and align with your values and passions.

Cultivate Gratitude and Positivity

Cultivate gratitude and positivity by focusing on the blessings and abundance in your life. Practice gratitude journaling, mindfulness, or acts of kindness to cultivate a positive mindset and appreciation for the present moment. Cultivating gratitude and positivity enhances your overall well-being and fosters a sense of fulfillment and contentment.

Embrace Growth and Learning

Embrace growth and learning as lifelong pursuits. Stay curious, open-minded, and willing to explore new ideas, experiences, and opportunities for personal and professional development. Continuously seek out opportunities for growth and self-improvement, and challenge yourself to step out of your comfort zone and expand your horizons.

Make a Difference

Find ways to make a positive impact on the world around you. Whether it's through volunteering, mentoring, advocacy, or acts of kindness, find ways to contribute your time, talents, and resources to causes that align with your values and passions. Making a difference not only benefits others but also brings a sense of purpose and fulfillment to your own life.

Conclusion

Living a life of purpose and fulfillment is a journey of self-discovery, growth, and contribution to the world. By clarifying your values and passions, setting meaningful goals, taking purposeful action, cultivating gratitude and positivity, embracing growth and learning, and making a difference in the lives of others, you can create a life that reflects your deepest aspirations and brings you joy, meaning, and fulfillment.

In the next chapter, we'll reflect on our journey of self-improvement and personal growth, celebrate our progress and accomplishments, and look towards the future with optimism and excitement. Through intentional action and a commitment to living with purpose and intention, we can create a life that is truly meaningful, fulfilling, and aligned with our highest values and aspirations.

CHAPTER TWENTY-NINE
REFLECTIONS ON THE JOURNEY
Focus: Celebrate Your Progress

As we near the end of our journey of self-improvement and personal growth, it's essential to take a moment to reflect on how far we've come, acknowledge the challenges we've faced, and celebrate the progress we've made. In this chapter, we'll reflect on our journey, celebrate our accomplishments, and look towards the future with optimism and excitement.

Looking Back on Your Progress

Take some time to reflect on the progress you've made on your journey of self-improvement and personal growth. Consider the goals you set for yourself, the obstacles you encountered along the way, and the steps you took to overcome them. Celebrate the milestones you've reached, no matter how small, and acknowledge the effort and dedication you've put into your personal development journey.

Acknowledging Challenges and Triumphs

Acknowledge the challenges you've faced on your journey and the lessons you've learned from them. Reflect on the moments of doubt, fear, and uncertainty you've experienced, and how you've persevered through them with courage and resilience. Celebrate the triumphs and successes you've achieved, no matter how small, and recognize the strength and determination it took to overcome obstacles and achieve your goals.

Planning for the Future

As you reflect on your journey, consider what lies ahead and the goals and aspirations you have for the future. Take some time to envision the life you want to create for yourself and the steps you need to take to make it a reality. Set new goals that inspire and challenge you, and create a plan of action to help you achieve them. Remember that personal growth is a lifelong journey. Look for new opportunities for learning, growth, and self-discovery.

Celebrating Your Journey

Celebrate the progress you've made, the lessons you've learned, and the person you've become along the way. Celebrate the courage, resilience, and determination you've demonstrated in pursuing your goals and aspirations. And most importantly, celebrate the journey itself, with all its ups and downs, twists and turns, joys and challenges.

Conclusion

Let us take a moment to reflect on how far we've come, acknowledge the challenges we've faced, and celebrate the progress we've made. Through introspection, perseverance, and a commitment to personal growth, we have embarked on a transformative journey of self-discovery and empowerment. Let us carry forward the lessons we've learned, the strengths we've developed, and the aspirations that inspire us. With a renewed sense of purpose and determination, we can continue to create a life that reflects our deepest values and aspirations, and make a positive impact on the world around us.

CHAPTER THIRTY
CONCLUSION: EMBRACING YOUR AWESOMENESS
Focus: You're a New You

As we stand at the threshold of this final chapter, it's time to reflect deeply on the profound journey we've undertaken together. Throughout this guide, we've delved into the intricacies of procrastination, grappled with the complexities of perfectionism, and embarked on a transformative voyage towards personal growth and self-empowerment. Now, as we bid farewell to this chapter, let us not only celebrate how far we've come but also embrace the boundless potential that lies within each of us.

Reflecting on Your Unique Journey

Take a moment to look back on the path you've traveled since the beginning of this guide. Recall the moments of doubt and uncertainty, the challenges you've faced, and the triumphs you've celebrated along the way. Reflect on the insights you've gained, the habits you've cultivated, and the changes you've implemented in pursuit of your goals. Your journey is as unique as you are, filled with twists and turns, setbacks and successes. Celebrate every step you've taken, knowing that each one has brought you closer to becoming the best version of yourself.

Committing to Lifelong Growth and Self-Improvement

As you reflect on your journey thus far, recommit yourself to the pursuit of lifelong growth and self-improvement. Embrace the idea that personal growth is not a destination but a journey—a journey that unfolds over a lifetime and offers endless opportunities for learning, exploration, and discovery. Set new goals that inspire and challenge you, knowing that each goal is a stepping stone on the path to realizing your full potential. Cultivate a mindset of curiosity, resilience, and openness to change, and embrace the journey with enthusiasm and determination.

Recognizing Your Inherent Awesomeness

Above all, remember that you are already awesome just as you are. Embrace your uniqueness, celebrate your strengths, and honor the journey that has brought you to this moment. You are a masterpiece in progress, a work of art in motion, capable of achieving greatness beyond your wildest dreams. Recognize the value that you bring to the world, the impact you have on those around you, and the potential you possess to create positive change in your life and the lives of others. Embrace your awesomeness with humility and grace, knowing that true greatness lies not in perfection but in authenticity, resilience, and the courage to be yourself.

Embracing the Journey Ahead

As we bring our journey to a close, let us look ahead with optimism, excitement, and anticipation for the adventures that lie ahead. The road ahead may be filled with challenges and uncertainties, but it is also brimming with opportunities and possibilities waiting to be explored. Embrace the journey with an open heart and an open mind, knowing that every experience, whether joyous or challenging, is an opportunity for growth and self-discovery. Trust in yourself, believe in your abilities, and know that you are capable of achieving anything you set your mind to.

Conclusion: The Journey Continues

As we bid farewell to this chapter of our lives, let us carry forward the lessons we've learned, the memories we've cherished, and the dreams we've dared to pursue. Let us continue to embrace our awesomeness with courage, compassion, and conviction, knowing that the journey towards self-improvement and personal growth is a lifelong endeavor. With each step we take, may we continue to inspire, uplift, and empower ourselves and those around us, leaving a legacy of positivity, resilience, and love in our wake. The journey continues, dear reader, and the best is yet to come. So, go forth with confidence, embrace your awesomeness, and let your light shine brightly for all the world to see.

ABOUT THE AUTHOR

Alexander Wellington is an author and speaker who has dedicated himself to helping individuals overcome procrastination and perfectionism. Growing up in a small town, Alexander discovered his passion for writing at a young age. However, he struggled with procrastination and perfectionism, hindering his creative endeavors.

Determined to break free from these obstacles, Alexander embarked on a personal journey of self-discovery and growth. Through years of introspection and trial and error, he began to unravel the patterns of behavior that held him back, ultimately discovering the keys to unlocking his full potential.

Now, Alexander shares his experiences and insights to inspire and empower others facing similar challenges. With a compassionate approach and relatable storytelling, he helps individuals embrace their unique gifts, pursue their passions with confidence, and create lives filled with meaning and fulfillment.

In his free time, Alexander enjoys exploring the outdoors and spending time with his family.